OCCASIONAL therapy™

FOR THE WEDDING

1

The Bride

OCCASIONAL therapy™

FOR THE WEDDING

9

SESSIONS FOR YOUR
SANITY AND SURVIVAL

DR. ELLYN GAMBERG

ELLIS & YOUNG PUBLISHING.
NEW YORK, NEW YORK

"For every minute you remain angry,
You give up sixty seconds of peace of mind."

—RALPH WALDO EMERSON

*This book is dedicated to every bride, groom,
parent, and sibling who has struggled with conflict
during a time filled with
excitement, joy, and change.*

M<small>Y DEEPEST THANKS</small> to my children, who give meaning to family celebrations and with love have taught me on many occasions that dancing through a happy life requires both letting go and holding on.

Much gratitude to my husband, who celebrates the value of my work and who encourages me to go confidently in the direction of my dreams.

With admiration to my mother, who has shown me that being strong strengthens children, families, and generations.

Great appreciation to my editor Paul whose talent and quiet humor helped me think ahead to the next page, to my designer Pauline whose creative abilities helped the words speak for themselves' and to my friend and colleague Sylvia whose professional contributions and encouragement were invaluable.

CONTENTS

INTRODUCTION

Getting Married Is Supposed to Be Wonderful, Right?

YOUR WEDDING DAY is just around the corner. You've sent out the invitations and selected (and reselected) your gown; all the details are falling into place. You've found the absolutely perfect location, you're narrowing down your list of florists, and your fiancé is looking into music for the reception. Most importantly, family, friends, and loved ones will be coming from far and wide to share the moment with you as you proclaim your commitment to the person with whom you will spend the rest of your life—who just happens to be your lover, partner, and best friend. If you're like most American women, you've had some vision of your dream wedding playing in your mind at many different times throughout your life. Now that it is your turn to get married, you have done everything within your power to ensure that your wedding will be perfect. So, then, everything must be great—right?

Perhaps not.

Most likely, you have pondered every last detail, made allowances for anything that could go wrong, talked endlessly with your friends, and hired a wedding planner. In short, you have factored everything into the equation—except your feelings. As a result—during what is supposed to be the most wonderful time of your life—you find that you are feeling less than wonderful. You may be paralyzed by the thought that your big day will be less than perfect. Or perhaps you are agitated, nervous, or overwhelmed one moment—and perfectly fine the next. You may feel like crying or pulling your hair out, or catch yourself pacing the apartment at 3 AM for no reason at all. Maybe you have just lashed out at a friend or relative who offered some unsolicited advice (*the nerve*), or you are freaking out because you have fallen a little behind with your "to do" list. Whatever the case, this is *not* how you should be feeling.

Although you are thrilled to be getting married, now that you have found your soul mate—and you haven't for a moment doubted your decision—you may be having some truly bad thoughts. You may find yourself feeling jealous of your single friends who aren't leaving the single life behind. And even though you have become the focus of constant attention from family, friends and relatives, there are days when you feel completely, utterly alone. Perhaps you feel depressed, even though you can't put your finger on exactly why, or—as you sense that your life is changing in monumental ways—you begin acting entitled, nasty, or just downright childish. If only there was a way to address these things.

Unfortunately, everything about planning a wedding seems to be removed from actually *living* the wedding. The entire "wedding industry" that has no doubt been courting you for some time (how did they find you, anyway?) is woefully unequipped to deal with these bigger issues. You can hire the best wedding planner, pour over the latest bridal magazines, spend way too much time hanging out at that website (you know the one), or talk away the hours on the phone with your friends, but none of this will solve the question to which you are dying to know the answer: *if getting married is supposed to be so great, why do I feel like this?*

You may have tried turning to your family and loved ones for advice, but you've probably already found that they can be of little help. In fact, even if you are from the most seemingly "normal" family (it's okay to pretend for a moment), the *stress* that surrounds the wedding may be affecting your own family members in some not-so-nice ways. Mom suddenly becomes obsessive in her need to remind you e-v-e-r-y d-a-y to call that florist. Little Sis picks this month, of all times, to enlist Mom and Dad's help in finding a new apartment. Or perhaps your family is getting caught up in more serious matters—anything from relatives who are not getting along, to so-and-so won't attend the reception if a particular person is there.

Well, at least you and your fiancé can work together to deal with some of these pressures. Actually, when was the last time the two of you had a serious conversation about anything? (Discussing possible table setting colors doesn't count here.) You may *believe* that together, as a couple, you are better able to deal with the stresses that accompany a wedding, yet this argument is better in theory than reality. If the two of you have talked about anything of substance lately, you will realize how many opposing personalities, concerns, and issues are tugging at each of you: your family would really like one detail to be included in the ceremony, his is lukewarm on the idea, you want him to be more involved in the planning, he feels that you wouldn't listen even if he did participate, etc.

As far as your families were concerned, when you were "just" dating, the relationship was your own business. Since you became engaged, it has become a family affair. You and he will realize—often abruptly—that now your relationship is "out there" for the family's discussion. Not only are you joining together as a couple, you are uniting two different families who will have to forge new relationships and new generations together. If there are children in the future (or, increasingly these days, already here), these children will be the descendants of both families and will most likely complicate the family dynamics. And naturally, at some point in the wedding planning, someone will turn to you and say something like, "At least you don't have to worry—it's your wedding, so everything must be great." Which, of course—given the way that you feel lately—is entirely maddening.

So what's going on here? Why are your family members picking this time, of all times, to act like this? Why has it become nearly impossible to talk with your fiancé, who is usually a source of support and comfort? While you would hope that everything go terrifically, events like a wedding may trigger unexpected emotions in you and those around you. Weddings are such a powerful force that they impact all involved; it's not because, for example, your family "has problems" or your fiancé doesn't care. Like other major family rituals, weddings are vehicles that transport a family's identity to future generations, providing family members with a sense of history and creating a connection to the future.

However, this movement can also be unsettling to emotions, relationships, and family dynamics as a whole. Some family members look at each other and reassess their relationships; others examine their own lives and react, and still others may be affected and not even realize it. Your fiancé may withdraw from the wedding process and become easily aggravated or argue with you about other things entirely as he comes to terms with his own personal issues or reservations. A parent or parents (either his or yours) may become saddened by the act of giving away their daughter (or "letting go" of their son). They may be facing a whole range of emotions as they come to terms with their changing roles in your lives and face their own transition into the next stage of life. As a result, they may sometimes overstep boundaries or get depressed themselves, even though they are happy for you. A younger sibling may feel like the family he grew up in is now dissolving; an older sibling may be reminded of her own failed marriage or reexamine his or her own life and see missed opportunities or experience other regrets. Friends and relatives may be affected—to a lesser extent—as they watch the boundaries of their relationships with you change.

There is no doubt that planning a wedding can be stressful. Just the sheer amount of details, money, and time involved can be overwhelming. However, you may be realizing that other feelings are surfacing that have nothing to do with wedding planning. If you have read this far, you are probably aware of the fact that there are deeper issues at play here—real issues that a whole army of wedding planners will never address. If these issues are not dealt with now, they *will* become magnified and affect future relationships with families, friends, and your partner. This book will help you face these issues now, before they get worse.

Occasional Therapy: Try It for the Wedding; Use It for Life

Occasional Therapy is for those people who need help on occasion. It is an eclectic approach to helping people, like you, who are otherwise well adjusted but are facing a difficult or troubling situation or time in their lives. Occasional Therapy combines the most powerful parts of a wide variety of therapeutic techniques. The exercises, techniques, and approaches presented in this book will allow you to become an active participant in your mental well-being and begin dealing with the uneasiness you are feeling. The best part about Occasional Therapy is that you will start learning strategies—today—that can help you *before* your wedding day. This book will allow you to work at your own pace, in the privacy of your own home. Occasional Therapy is *not* about spending endless amounts of time revisiting childhood problems. It *is* about learning clear, simple strategies to help you deal with the issues you are facing today.

Imagine learning an easy-to-use exercise that will have you relaxing— slowing down the rhythms of your breathing, putting a halt to the endless negative scripts that are running unchecked in your mind—and being able to harness this ability whenever you want. (You will find that in Session Five.) Or, how about some suggestions that you and your spouse can use—now—to get the most out of your conversations or find out the real reason behind your constant bickering of late? (No problem—turn to Session Nine.) Occasional Therapy will have you engaging in thoughts and verbal interaction to bring about self-knowledge and achieve clarification of feelings; it has been specifically created to alter behaviors and create improved interpersonal skills.

While the term Occasional Therapy is new, the theories that led to its development are not. Occasional Therapy is actually based on theories of **cognitive behavioral therapy**, a school of therapy that attempts to help people by modifying everyday thoughts and behaviors. Treatment is generally brief, time-limited, and very focused on the problems linked directly to the immediate stressor.

All clinical or otherwise unusual terms in this book are highlighted in **bold text** and then explained in-depth in the Glossary at the end of this book.

Occasional Therapy, like other forms of short-term therapy, is for people going through some change in their life, who are searching for a level of balance or acceptance with the environment, others, or themselves. Short-term therapies in general, like Occasional Therapy, are a time-tested, respected approach to dealing with the stark realities of situational events.

If you thought that reading this book would involve months or years of your time, or meant dredging up painful memories, would you be reading this right now? I thought not—and I designed Occasional Therapy with this in mind. Actually, reading *Occasional Therapy for the Wedding* and utilizing the strategies taken from short-term therapy models may be the best hope in reaching people like you: ones who really need help—now! Instead of discussing all aspects of your past (and present) life, the brief **psychotherapy** techniques offered in *Occasional Therapy for the Wedding* seek to empower you while generating a few simple solutions. Reading *Occasional Therapy for the Wedding* will maximize the limited amount you have to work with, through the easy-to-use, clear strategies that I will provide throughout the book. I will not trot out endless stories about brides I have counseled or other cute anecdotes. I know that you are here to help yourself, and *Occasional Therapy for the Wedding* was written with you in mind.

Please note: *Occasional Therapy for the Wedding* offers strategies, exercises, and suggestions regarding a specific problem—in particular, a looming "lifecycle event" such as a wedding (you may also find these helpful in coping with other lifecycle events such as the birth of a baby or retirement). Reading *Occasional Therapy for the Wedding* will also be helpful if you wonder if your particular situation and reactions to it are normal. Participating in individual psychotherapy will be a better bet if you want to understand your patterns of behavior and how they developed, or if you have had repeated difficulties with family and intimate relationships. Seeking the help of your own mental health care professional is *absolutely* essential if you are suicidal, psychotic, or suffer from a condition requiring medication.

I Don't Really Need This Book, Do I?

My question back to you is: *what is the alternative?*

When confronted with a difficult situation, most people will automatically, unconsciously draw upon past experiences when responding. These familiar past experiences, emotions, or situations have become the basis for patterns of behavior that are repeated over and over again—whether or not they work.

But what about the decisions required by a completely new experience, like those involved in a wedding? When faced with a new, challenging situation or an unfamiliar emotion for which you have no past frame of reference, you will probably become uncomfortable and (like most of us) feel the need to share your pain or confusion with a loved one. You may turn to a friend, parent, significant other, sibling, or other trusted person for advice or comfort. Yet too many times, it is precisely these people who are either involved in the troubling situation, causing the situation, or have little or no experience dealing with the situation. (Asking your brother—a lifelong bachelor—for advice on commitment issues would fall under this category.)

Reading *Occasional Therapy for the Wedding* will allow you to focus on yourself without the distraction of others' opinions, criticisms, or judgments. The supportive, therapeutic suggestions made here will provide you with the freedom needed to look inside yourself and discover your own insights and solutions. Through experience, I have found that most people who are determined to resolve the issues for which they seek professional help are capable of resolving their own problems. You are no different.

You're Going to Need More Than Aromatherapy to Get Through This One

In our modern-day lives, our own individual expectations, family pressures, and societal demands are so tremendous that from time-to time—particularly around demanding events—our lives are filled with confusion, conflict, frustration, and disappointment. Since we live in a society used to instant gratification, driven by limited time, and dependent on such conveniences as on-demand television, high-speed Internet, and same-day dry-cleaning, most of us have come to want things fixed quickly—including our problems. However, attending to our personal well-being and health often comes last on our list, if at all; finding the time to fit in a dentist appointment, go to the gym, or attend a friend's birthday party becomes a hassle. As much as it might be needed, engaging in weeks of psychotherapy may be out of the question.

The pace of our lives has become so fast that we have kidded ourselves into believing just about anything with instant gratification can be emotionally therapeutic. The once exclusively clinical term "therapy" has taken on a new meaning. People today refer to anything that makes them feel better as therapy—"retail therapy," "chocolate therapy," "spa therapy"—the list goes on. These all can be helpful and relaxing to help get through tough choices and rough days, but the real underlying issues are left to fester, untouched. The concept of Occasional Therapy is therapy for today's world: it strikes a balance between the realities of our need-it-yesterday society and the necessity of finding solutions that will produce long-term, tangible results.

Why do you Advocate Occasional Therapy?

Quite honestly, as my children began to marry, I needed some "occasional therapy" for these events in my own life. As I watched and participated in the wedding planning, feelings of childbirth surfaced over and over again. It was a moment that I knew was coming for months, yet, with both excitement and fear I worried and wondered what my new role would be like—and how my family would change. Likewise, I realized that their lives were changing as they took this next big step into adulthood. Having spent over twenty years of my life working with patients suffering from **adjustment** and **anxiety disorders**, I knew that lifecycle events could trigger emotions that are often deeply buried. But, *knowing* and *feeling* are two different things. Now that it was my family, I was out of sorts. From time to time, everyone (even psychologists, psychiatrists, and psychotherapists) will face challenges and changes in their lives that can be extremely difficult. Even at the most joyous of times, each of us still can feel anxious, nervous, and afraid.

Although the situations are different from family to family, frustrations and anxieties make people behave irrationally and unreasonably. **Stress** (for a clinical definition, see the Glossary) makes people tired and teary; fear makes others nervous and apprehensive; "what-ifs" can became obsessions. As a parent, I can relate to the change and confusion that occurs as personal roles shift and new family dynamics unfurl. As a professional—and in my personal life too—I have learned that shifting perspectives, recognizing mistakes, and trying to practice forgiveness can heal many wounds. Although events such as the wedding can test the strength of families and may tug on the heartstrings of parents and children, they also present an opportunity for families to work through their issues together and make room for the next generation and all the good it will bring.

How to Use This Book

You will find this book to be enjoyable to read and easy to use. It will help you learn how to ask—and answer—the questions that your wedding has no doubt unearthed. *Occasional Therapy for the Wedding* provides exercises, strategies, and techniques you can start using now, and it allows you to take an active role in your own psychological growth.

This book is divided into chapters for each member of the wedding party. (Don't worry, I know that you brides need extra attention, and I have lots of extra information devoted to you.) You will want to read the other chapters to understand better what your loved ones are going through (and who wouldn't want to eavesdrop on their betrothed's therapy session?) Also, you will probably find it helpful to keep a notebook on hand to jot down your own personal notes along the way. Each chapter begins with some *background* and then quickly moves to *symptoms* (you know, the reasons you picked up this book in the first place). *Presenting problems*, the deeper issues most likely bringing about those symptoms, are then discussed in detail. Throughout the "Problems" section, I offer techniques that you can begin using now, alone or with your partner, parents, siblings, or friends. I don't pretend to have all the answers to every question; not every problem or issue has a corresponding exercise, and some have several. And that's exactly the point: you will see that with Occasional Therapy, sometimes the best exercise is to simply be *aware* of the issue. I have included some additional exercises in several chapters ("Something to Think About") and at the end of each chapter, I have included some *insights*, thoughts assembled after twenty-plus years of doing this.

Most importantly, you will learn about your own behaviors and how you can actively change when faced with events in your life. Reading *Occasional Therapy for the Wedding* will help you figure out how to survive the wedding and enjoy it,—and will provide you with insights into yourself that will help you cope with other occasional events (the pregnancy, the in-law holiday visits, or the birth of a child, for example).

What's next? Set aside some time and find a quiet place that is yours alone. Get comfortable in your favorite chair and relax your mind and your body. Read carefully and enjoy at your own pace. You are closer than you think to that wedding you have always dreamed about.

1

PRIVATE THOUGHTS

Going Out of My Mind

BACKGROUND

*H*OW ARE YOU feeling lately? (How much time do I have, right?)

Most likely, your moods are alternating between overwhelmed, tired, excited, and confused, or perhaps you are elated one day and sad the next. You may be arguing with your family and avoiding your spouse—or vice versa. Whatever the particulars of your situation, you don't understand why you are feeling like this. If this is supposed to be the happiest time of your life, no one told you.

If you are like most brides, you are having a difficult time picturing what you will look like wearing a veil, whether a striped tux shirt really makes sense on your groom—not to mention trying to figure out if those orchid and rose centerpieces will "fit" with the rest of the room. So how can you possibly envision what your new life will be like? You are not only preparing to be diva (princess, queen, etc.) for a day, but you are also stepping into a much more profound role as a "wife" (and along with it, daughter-in-law, and maybe throw in sister in-law too, for life). Your new life will be more complicated in many ways. Just for starters, you must figure out living arrangements, shared finances, and career plans, and perhaps even think about starting a family. I know that these changes can be scary—even if you are lucky enough to get along your new family.

And if you are like most brides, there is probably some sort of personal "drama" involving your loved ones. This can range from anything to Mom offering unsolicited advice (how many times has she commented on your choice of appetizers?), to your younger sister, who picks now (really, why *now?*) to break up with her new boyfriend, to your friends—who, when they aren't telling you how to do things, are way-too-happily recalling their own families' wedding horror stories. Most likely, your fiancé is dealing with pressures from his family—from his mother, who feels that she's getting left out of the decision making, to bickering relatives of his own.

Consider yourself lucky if the situations above describe you. Some readers may be dealing with a mother who is reliving her own wedding experience and wants her daughter's wedding to be the fancy wedding she never had, or a sister who may be wishing it was she that was getting married. Some of you will be faced with a groom who could just care less about the wedding planning or friends putting out negative vibes because they are worried that you won't be around as much anymore.

And let's face it: weddings in general have become more complicated affairs these days. For many of us, there are hurdles to navigate—both logistical and personal—that come with uniting two people from different religious, racial, or cultural backgrounds. Perhaps you are trying to plan a nonreligious wedding or some sort of other alternative affair—how is your family reacting to that decision? Or maybe the two of you are trying to avoid all these hassles and elope? Good luck: now you must face the hurt feelings and emotions of family members and friends who are saddened with the thought of being left out of your special moment.

So what's really going on here? This "wedding **anxiety**" is really about change—and to some extent, adjusting to the psychological process of leaving your old life behind and beginning a new life. The unknown is hitting you now, big time, with a very real form of anticipatory stress—and you worry (consciously or not) about how you will cope with the changed dynamics, responsibilities and duties that marriage will bring. Like many of the other major life events, the wedding may actually require an **adjustment** (or many). And if you have read this far, you know that Occasional Therapy—like any good therapy—can help.

Please don't get offended if I tell you that you are probably already spending way too much time on the details of your wedding. Taking the little bit of time that it requires to slow down and attempt to understand the thoughts that are racing through your head, and your new role(s) in life, is well worth it. I don't have to tell you that doing this self-exploration now, before the wedding, is much more helpful than afterward.

Symptoms

There are many signs and symptoms that you may notice when you are experiencing stress and **anxiety**. These signs and symptoms fall into four categories: feelings, thoughts, behavior, and physiology. When you are under stress, it is not unusual to experience one or more of the following:

FEELINGS

- Feeling anxious
- Feeling edgy
- Feeling scared
- Feeling nervous
- Feeling irritable
- Feeling wound up
- Feeling moody
- Feeling alarmed

THOUGHTS

- Low self-esteem
- Fear of failure
- Inability to concentrate
- Worrying about the future
- Embarrassing easily
- Preoccupation with thoughts and tasks

BEHAVIOR

- Stuttering and other speech difficulties
- Crying for no apparent reason
- Acting impulsively
- Startling easily
- Grinding your teeth
- Increasing smoking; use of drugs and alcohol
- Becoming accident-prone
- Losing your appetite or overeating

PHYSIOLOGY

- Perspiration or sweaty hands
- Trembling
- Dryness of throat and mouth
- Tiring easily
- Diarrhea, indigestion, and vomiting

The following are some of the most common symptoms I observe in my private practice with brides-to-be:

OVERWHELMED

- Feeling like there's too much to do and too little time to do it.
- Trying to juggle the balancing act—your job, wedding planning, family pressures, and more.
- Worrying about the looming financial pressures.

EATING TOO MUCH—OR NOT ENOUGH

- Binge eating, eating too much (generally unhealthy and not good for getting into that gown on the big day).
- Not eating enough: good for fitting into your gown—and just about nothing else.

NOT SLEEPING

- Not sleeping frees up some time to address envelopes in the middle of night, but it won't help with the circles under your eyes.
- Feeling tired or fatigued in general.

ANXIETY

- The feeling that something's going wrong, though you're not quite sure what "something" is.
- Just plain feeling "overloaded" with things to do.
- Having **panic attacks**, feeling like you can't breathe, waking up freaking out and thinking that you're dying (I've had patients tell me that even if you die, your caterer gets to keep your deposit).
- Worried that you'll have to give up your girlfriends and chick flicks.
- Nervous that something or someone will be left out of something, or that a major wedding detail will be overlooked.

FEAR OF . . . JUST ABOUT EVERYTHING

- Similar to **anxiety** but based on some bad feeling or incident that you have experienced in the past.
- Concerned someone actually won't have a good time at the wedding (impossible), a family member or friends will not approve of your decisions (quite likely), or you might say something to offend the wedding planner—and he will quit and then what!

SADNESS

- Alternating between feeling up—then down—about leaving the single life behind, giving up your lifestyle, becoming monogamous.
- Scared that you're leaving behind the life you've grown to love, and that you may, finally—get ready—be growing up.

ANGER

- Where can we start? Your family is acting anything-but friendly, your groom couldn't care less, Mom is getting way too involved—wait, that's how they've always been.
- No one seems to agree with any of your decisions.
- No one is doing what you asked him or her to do—or he or she is not doing it fast enough.

SELF-ABSORBED

- This wedding is all about me—I'm not interested in anything else right now.
- Having a fit or temper tantrum when a vendor doesn't return your call fast enough.
- Everyone wants you to make this about "them"—when it is "your day."

IRRATIONAL FEELINGS OR ACTIONS

- Blowing things out of proportion.
- Alternating between "every last detail about this wedding has to be perfect" to "when will this be over?"
- Feeling "things are going too well, something must be wrong."

PRESENTING PROBLEMS

Conflict Over Wedding Details

Try to hear me out before reacting, okay?

Although the wedding is all about you, it involves decisions that will in some way impact everyone involved and everyone attending.

Your wedding represents not only the union of two distinct personalities, sets of opinions, and gender roles, but also of two families with differing backgrounds, cultures, and issues. Think back to what it may have involved to pick out paint colors for the living room (if you are already cohabitating) or the energy it took to decide where to go on that first vacation away together—when it was just the two of you. Now here you are making decisions that will matter to an entire group of people; you and your loved ones (whoever "they" may be) will have to live with these decisions. Traditionally, you, the bride, are worried about the caterer, flowers, gowns, bridal dresses, etc. (read: *everything*), and you have given your groom the tasks of finding a band and managing honeymoon plans (you can wait until you put down this book to remind him about these things—again). However, as you and your mate begin checking items off your "to do" list, every action seems to be interrelated. Your family wants things done a certain way; his might be less vocal—sometimes so much so that it is hard to figure out if you are getting the silent treatment, or if they even care at all! And of course, your friends typically check in with some brutally honest declarations—but then again, you're used to that.

The following exercise may help you deal with some of these issues.

Practice Better Communciation Skills

The wedding is a good opportunity to test your communication and resolution skills by listening, asking clarifying questions, speaking clearly and non-defensively, and then working toward negotiating a "creative alternative" or compromise solution.

Try To:

- Start with the easy issues.
- Define the issues as emotional versus factual.
- Identify the difficult issues.
- Prioritize the issues for both sides.
- Think before you speak.

- Be specific in stating what you believe the problem is.
- Ask for feedback on the major points from your mate—don't go into this with blinders on.
- Confine your remarks and comments to only one point at a time (create a list if you have to).
- Restate the opposing positions for clarity.
- Find areas of agreement.
- Determine concessions that both parties can make.
- Create options and monitor responses.
- Consider a compromise.
- Encourage each other.

Try Not To:

- Threaten
- Sabotage
- Bully
- Label or name-call
- Issue ultimatums
- Complain or whine—it is so easy to slip into that childhood voice.
- Assume that you know why the other person is responding the way he or she is (you are not a mind reader).
- "Correct" how someone else feels (always validate and acknowledge his or her feelings—those feelings are just as valuable as yours).
- Talk about the past; the problem exists now—deal with it in the present.

 ### Get Down to Basics

Spend time with an old friend and do some of the favorite things that you used to do together before you became "a bride." This will help you get in touch with the old feelings and memories of you before this life changing relationship.

Confusion About Everything and Everybody

Right now, you are probably confused about everything: trying to figure out who you are as a person, where your life is going, and *who are these people that I thought I knew?* The entire wedding experience may be raising questions about who your parents are as adults and as "people"—let alone these siblings whom you shared a bedroom with for thirteen years. All of a sudden, the people you thought you knew have become strangers or are just acting strangely. However, even if you are confused about things, you look in the mirror and see the same girl you always were (well, maybe a little more pale and tired). And although most brides perceive themselves as "being the same person they always were," typically, those close to them have a different opinion.

Reconnect With Your Past

Take some time out for yourself. Be selfish; it's okay. Call an old friend you haven't seen in a while, or pick up an activity or hobby you put on hold when the wedding madness began. And try to remember that friendship is based on a reciprocal sharing and common interests. If you are like many brides-to-be, you may have the tendency to get so wrapped up in the wedding plans that you temporarily lose the ability to relate to your friends . . . so try to figure out whether your friends have a reason for withdrawing from you lately. Keep in mind that, sure, your friends love you, but they may not necessarily have that same, limitless love (called **unconditional positive regard**) that a parent does. Put things in perspective: can you blame your friends if they're not enthralled with your tales of finding a chef who can bake a sublime pink soufflé?

Anxiety Over Fear of Commitment

Sure, you are committed to making your marriage work, and you know that you have found your soul mate. So then, what are you so afraid of?

The feeling that "this is it" can be petrifying. Whatever the root cause, you are feeling a huge pressure to make your marriage work, which in your mind now becomes making the wedding "work." For some brides, anything that does not go smoothly or which poses some sort of a threat to upsetting the planning process can elicit all sorts of irrational fears. Perhaps you have had problems committing to relationships in the past. Maybe you have been married before, or he has, or your parents are divorced. At the very least, you have heard how many marriages in our country end in divorce and wonder what is going wrong for so many couples.

Regardless of what is making you feel this way, it is important to ask, "What about commitment am I really afraid of?" Being committed to the wrong person? Being committed to anyone in general? Maybe it's the institution of marriage in general that is scaring you? Usually, just taking the time to follow through and see where those thoughts lead is enough.

When you feel yourself having these fears, it is important to remain on track. The following ideas will help.

Recognize Your Patterns and Apply **Behavior Modification** Techniques

Think about all the other commitments you have made in your life: leaving home to attend college, accepting a new job, signing the lease on your first apartment, etc. Now, try to remember what any one of those felt like. Was the experience really as bad as your knee jerk reaction would make you think? In reality, weren't some, perhaps all, of those feelings associated with these events actually good? Thinking for yourself in situations like this can be very reassuring when you look back and realize that you have made some very competent decisions on your own. Consider the following:

Think and Talk About Yourself POSITIVELY

- Eliminate adding qualifying statements to your opinions or requests ("You'll probably think this is crazy, but—," "I guess," or "But that's just my opinion").
- Try to stop using tag questions ("Does that make sense?" or "Is that okay?").

Consciously Take Responsibility for Yourself and Avoid Taking Responsibility for Others

- Eliminate "should," "ought to," and "have to" from your vocabulary.
- Practice using the phrase "I choose to."

Is there a certain pattern you are recognizing? Perhaps there is. Perhaps each time you faced a monumental decision, instead of acting—or reacting—you froze, did nothing, and got depressed. If that pattern caused you unpleasantness or sadness or was just plain ineffective, it is good to recognize that fact now. You can learn from your mistakes and this time, try not to repeat the pattern. Don't feel embarrassed or ashamed; everyone makes mistakes. No one is perfect. If thinking back to that time elicits scary or other negative feelings—like those similar to what you are feeling now—that is good, too. How did you deal with them then? Did you often deal with these feelings this way? Ask for help and support.

Thought Awareness

Thought awareness is the process by which you observe your thoughts for a time, perhaps when under stress, and you become aware of what is going through your head. Examples of some common negative thoughts are:

- Worries about how you appear to other people: *"They will think I'm stupid."*
- A preoccupation with the symptoms of stress: *"I can't stop thinking about how tense my shoulders are."*

- Dwelling on consequences of poor performance: *"If the wedding isn't perfect, my parents will be so disappointed."*
- Self-criticism: *"I am not a beautiful bride."*
- Feelings of inadequacy: *"I'll never be able to make all the right decisions."*

Rational Thinking

Once you are aware of your negative thoughts, write them down and review them rationally. Do the thoughts have any basis in reality?

POSITIVE THINKING AND AFFIRMATION

YOU MAY FIND it useful to counter negative thoughts with positive affirmations. You can use affirmations to build confidence and change negative behavior patterns into positive ones. Some examples of affirmations are:

- "I can do this."
- "I can achieve my goals."
- "I am completely myself, and people will like me for myself."
- "I am completely in control of my life."
- "I learn from my mistakes. They increase the basis of experience on which I can draw."
- "I am a good, valued person in my own right."

Decide rationally what goals you can realistically attain with hard work, and then use positive thinking to reinforce these.

Identifying the fears you associated with the idea of "commitment" will go a long way toward eliminating them. You can become empowered by learning to replace problem thoughts and maladaptive behaviors with more constructive ways of thinking and acting.

Fear of "Growing Up"

For many brides, when it hits them that they are finally growing up, moving on, and becoming an adult—which can mean different things to each of us—it can be pretty tough. Weddings and other significant transitions can trigger many childhood fears to emerge. Sometimes the results aren't pretty: just ask those around . . . never mind, trust me. The part that emerges is the part that feels like a little girl or boy, the part that needs nurturing, caring, security and affection, the part that still carries the pain, trauma, disappointments, and hurt from childhood.

As young children, we learn to protect ourselves from emotional pain and unpleasant feelings. Early on, we learn **defense mechanisms** to help us cope. These can take the following forms:

Projection is a defense mechanism where people hide their own threatening impulses by placing them on other people. (*You've heard it before—"It's not me—it's everyone else that is. . . ."*)

Mom's the one obsessing over everything—I'm just going to make sure I tell everyone in the family that she's obsessing over everything. Fifteen times.

Rationalization occurs when people are not able to deal with the real reasons they are behaving in a particular way; they protect themselves by making up logical explanations for their behaviors. (*It makes us sound so logical and smart when we can offer that "reasonable" explanation.*)

It's okay to be completely rude to every last vendor—I'm paying a lot of money for this wedding!

Regression happens when people are faced with a situation that makes them so anxious or nervous they often protect themselves by retreating to an earlier stage of development. *(It sounds so childish, but the next time the dressmaker or florist throws a "tantrum," you will get it.)*

My friend invited everyone—but me—to join her for her tenth gown fitting. I don't even want to go to her wedding. I would rather stay home by myself.

Denial is unconsciously attempting to resolve emotional conflict and to reduce anxiety by refusing to acknowledge the more unpleasant, perhaps painful reality. *(There is no way that my bridesmaids would refuse to all wear the same shoes, and there is no way that my fiancé's mother would not go along with the idea of. . . . You can fill this one in yourself.)*

Try to recognize which defense mechanisms you are using. You may be making an unconscious effort to avoid, face, or accept the real issue that is hurtful. If you are being accused by others that you are in constant denial, or if you are rationalizing everything, ask yourself whether there is any truth in what they are saying. Are you avoiding something painful?

How Grown Up Are You Really?

Ask yourself if you really see yourself as the person that he, your fiancé, and others see. And ask yourself if you are being honest with yourself—or have you become what others want you to be? The wedding may be a time that you find yourself trying to please everyone and not feeling so good about yourself.

Try asking yourself just exactly what type of bride you are. Doing this can help you gain insight into your current behavior. If you are acting childishly, maybe you aren't ready to handle some of the adult responsibilities that are facing you, and in some way your family still needs to be involved to "rescue" you. Maybe adolescent behaviors are resulting in conflict with your parents and their desire to control—and yours to rebel. Perhaps who you are is not an issue, and you are exhibiting a high level of maturity.

How do you see yourself?

- **The little girl:** Someone who needs to be nurtured and cared for; someone who can be dependent and afraid to be alone. Oftentimes this is someone who needs to be rescued from her own family or who has been abandoned in some way.
- **The high school cheerleader:** A little more grown-up—someone who will cheer her man on through life and view him as her hero—but perhaps not quite mature enough to make decisions on her own, or is still being controlled by her parents and influenced by her friends
- **The independent woman:** Someone who is ready for commitment and ready to share her life with someone else. This kind of maturity allows each person to grow independently and yet become entwined with each other's life—as opposed to being enmeshed to the point of giving up who he or she is.

Maybe by identifying what part of your childhood is "acting out" right now, you can better understand some of your feelings.

The "type" of bride you are may also have a lot to do with how you are handling your new roles and responsibilities lately. Each bride "type" usually feels conflicted and confused as a result of the amount of interaction they have with their families, their unique style, and their traditional (or not so traditional) beliefs.

- **Traditional princess bride:** A (usually) young woman with parents active in the planning and financing of an once-in-a lifetime, fairy-tale wedding.
- **Traditional independent bride:** Financially independent, she plans her own wedding (often with the groom's help); the independent bride respects tradition but adds her own unique style.
- **Nontraditional independent bride:** Typically marries later in life—or was married before; usually plans a small, nontraditional wedding. Nontraditional brides are very common in second marriages and blended families.

Get in Touch With Your Inner Child Bride

As adults, we often do not acknowledge that the experiences and feelings we had as children are still alive and kicking within us and are a legitimate part of who we have become. Instead, we spend a lifetime trying to ignore this part of ourselves. We may be afraid that if we acknowledge the kid within us, bad memories might resurface; we might experience pain, weakness, or otherwise feel powerless—and we are somehow less of an adult. Finding, recognizing and acknowledging our inner child can actually give us the freedom to grow up.

Psychologists refer to this as "inner child work," and identifying what "type" of bride you really are can help you to get in touch with your feelings. Many times, childhood dreams, fantasies, and expectations are responsible for your view of the wedding, the image of what a bride should be, and (of course) what your Prince Charming will look like. Even if you are the most successful, professional "adult," you may not want to wake up from your dream or let go of whatever part of your childhood gave you that memory. If that describes you, ask yourself—*What kind of bride am I?*

Yet, if we instead try to embrace this side of us, we can accept our disappointments and begin to heal our inner child's pain, doubts, or weaknesses. After this, we can address the negative feelings of insecurity or mistrust that were developed as a child and heal them, thereby stopping them from negatively interfering in our adult life. Making the effort to admit to the fact that your child within is a valid part of your personality, you will take the first powerful step toward reevaluating negative feelings and substituting them with positive ones.

REGRESS A LITTLE

*M*AYBE YOU ARE uncertain about who should be included in the bridal procession, or how to respond to your fiancé's request to invite a troublesome relative—and need a way to work it out. Try the following:

continued

Imagine yourself as a small child in a situation where you felt overwhelmed or uncertain. It will be helpful if you can pick a situation that may relate in some way to your wedding (i.e., whom should you invite to your sweet-sixteen party . . . or giving the speech at your graduation).

Think back and remember what you thought about yourself (*I am too weak to speak up, I am so stupid, I should be able to figure this out, etc.*). Now, remember a time as an adult that you were put in a similar situation and handled it well.

Today, whenever those "childish" feelings emerge, take a deep breath and tell yourself that the adult part of you is strong and capable, and that it will protect that very vulnerable child within. In other words, when the negative, childish feelings surface, they will be acknowledged and then be taken over by the strong adult you are now.

Remember, it is okay, probably even healthy—and most certainly fun—to indulge your inner child bride for a bit. However, the adult you are now should be in control of most of the wedding planning, and certainly your marriage. As with anything else—when we learn more about ourselves, it is important to be aware of what is happening with our thoughts.

Some Things to Think About

Actually, therapists call this "homework," but I know that you never would have read this far if I gave the section that title.

Still with me? However you refer to this section, working on yourself is some of the most important work you can do. The following exercises should give you some easy-to-use practical tips on ferreting out some of the feelings we haven't yet addressed. Start by taking the quick self-assessment in number one below. Answer each question honestly, even if it hurts a little. The goal here is to look critically at yourself to try to figure out what is really going on with *you*—not with you and your fiancé, not with you and your mother, and not with you and the caterer.

A QUICK SELF-ASSESSMENT

Why Am I Feeling Like This?

Try to look at the possible causes of your behavior. This can help you see some of the reasons for your behavior. Did they always exist? Do they exist because of something to do with your thinking? Perhaps you are feeling or acting this way because you are not getting enough rest. Consider the following, and acknowledge the truth:

- **Long-term predisposing:** Have you always felt like this? Maybe everyone in your family acts like this. Maybe your behavior is heredity, or from childhood, or from cumulative stress.
- **Biological:** It could be something deeper. Maybe a medically-based or organic cause for why you might be having panic attacks or bouts of depression.
- **Short-term triggering:** Perhaps now is when all the past personal losses, life changes, and trauma you have experienced as a child are "set off" by some similar events happening to you now.
- **Maintaining:** Your mind can run away with you. (That's okay— as long as you are back in time for the wedding.) Sometimes we base our decisions and actions on mistaken beliefs. Often a lack of assertiveness and a lack of purpose stop us from moving forward when we are overwhelmed.
- **Assess your physical levels:** Only *you* know how you really feel inside. You can hide the dark circles under yours eyes, but you might feel exhausted. Everyone may say you look fabulous since you dropped those ten pounds. They don't know it's because you are sick to your stomach and too nervous and upset to eat.

Add your own here:

_____

_____

_____

_____

_____

What Sorts of Thoughts Have You Been Having Lately?

People often create their own anxiety by generating negative statements that they repeat over and over, eventually leading to worst-case scenario, "what if" statements.

- *What if the cake is not the flavor I ordered?*
- *What if my sister's boyfriend wears white socks?*
- *What if Dad slips and mentions some embarrassing story about my in-laws he wasn't supposed to know?*

Learning to recognize and acknowledge these negative thoughts when you have them is the first step to ridding yourself of them. Once you have recognized the statement, immediately try to make a counter statement that is positive in nature:

What if my cake is not the flavor I ordered? *It probably won't happen, and I will handle it if it does. (Everyone will still eat and love it no matter what flavor it is.)*

LOOK HOW YOU HAVE BEEN BEHAVING!

OVER THE CENTURIES, theorists have described people as falling into types, or categories, of personality, each with distinct behaviors. How we view ourselves plays an important factor in how we behave, how we view the world, and how others view us.

Look at how you have been acting lately; it might give you some insight into why others are seeing you differently lately, or why you are feeling differently about yourself.

❑ **The Narcissist:** *Is this all about you!* A narcissist acts out of self-love. People may think you are behaving as one, but really—is it self-love or is it love of the perfect wedding?

Does this sound like you?

"This is my special day, and everyone else must realize that; I am due the special attention and deserve special treatment."

Maybe you are just acting *entitled*.

❑ **The Control Freak:** Has your credo become, *"If you want it done, do it yourself,"* or have you always been a control freak? Wanting everything to be predictable, you can't let go and trust; therefore, you must make sure you do everything right yourself or see to it personally that it is done. If this is typical of you, no one will be offended, but if its not, then maybe you understand why you are so stressed out.

❑ **The Victim:** *Woe is me!* Feeling or acting helpless, hopeless, or that no progress can be made will only put you behind (and there is so much to do). *Wedding victims* often believe something is wrong with them; either they are deprived or unworthy, or perhaps there are always obstacles between them and their goals. Like all victims, you be careful not to promote sadness and depression in others.

❑ **The Pessimist:** *If it can go wrong to anyone, I know it will happen to me* (at least, that is what you think). Always imagining the worst-case scenario, and having fantasies of disaster, doom, and gloom, can bring on psychosomatic illness. The pessimist is very good at promoting anxiety, onto herself and those around her.

❑ **The Critic:** *Picky! Picky! Picky!*—Go pick on someone else other than yourself. Always judging or evaluating your own behavior is not good for your overall wedding (not to mention yourself after the marriage). Although you may be an expert at pointing out your own flaws, your critic skill can be put to much better use. The critic is very good at promoting low self-esteem.

continued

❑ **The Perfectionist:** Everyone knows you want everything to be perfect—and I am sure many people think you are perfect. They will think your wedding is perfect. But if nothing is ever good enough, if nothing less than 100 percent is acceptable, you will have perfect unhappiness. If you push unreasonably hard to reach your goals, you will have achieved perfection in promoting chronic stress.

Does this sound like you?

"Everything must be exactly so; nothing can deviate from how I want it. Mistakes, miscalculations, technical, or human errors are not an option!"

What's Really On Your Mind?

Like the lyrics to a song we just can't get out of our head, messages and repeated thoughts will run through our minds, like it or not. These repetitive thoughts can translate into repetitive actions, oftentimes based upon scripts we have learned early on in our lives. As we grow up and learn right from wrong, good from bad, what is important, and what is unimportant, phrases such as "you should always" and "you should never" are implanted firmly in our brains. These same messages often surface when you are in conflict or in uncertainty. So, when you find yourself conflicted by a thought that you feel really is not your own, stop and figure out where this script came from (your parents, a teacher, etc.). This will help you realize *who told me to believe this or think this way, or where have I heard this before?*

Now think about it: is it really you thinking these thoughts, or has someone momentarily 'kidnapped' your brain?

By doing this exercise you should be able to figure out "whose" voice keeps running through your head (your mother's, your father's, the voice of an old schoolteacher). Once you have identified that person—you can freely "speak up" for yourself. In your own voice, of course.

The Empty Chair

As the wedding planning has probably made you notice, sometimes the hardest part about a perceived conflict is getting up the nerve to speak to someone. This exercise may just give you that push you need.

> Pretend that the person you are about to confront, apologize to, disappoint, etc., is sitting in a chair in front of you. Start speaking in the present tense and begin having a dialogue—pretending that you are both people. (You'll probably want to try this one when no one else is around.) Respond to your own comments as you expect the other person might. Continue the dialogue, being honest and being prepared for all the actual arguments and responses you predict that the other person will make. You are free to say things that perhaps you would never "really" say, just take this opportunity to "let it all out." This can help to release a lot of pent-up feelings, and for some can actually be a **catharsis**. At other times, this technique will be useful for problem solving and identifying feelings and thoughts that are blocking a healthy relationship or positive outcomes in your own personal life.

Visualize Your Wedding

Visualization is the process through which your mind processes and stores information. In this exercise, you will use your mind's natural visualization processes to help you reduce anxiety and relax. You will do this by repeatedly visualizing yourself in a situation where the outcome is one you desire, one that will help you reach your goals.

Visualization can be a very refreshing and pleasant way of meditating. Here you will create a mental image of a pleasant and relaxing place in your mind. Involve all your senses in the imagery: see the place, hear the sounds, smell the aromas, feel the temperature and the movement of the wind. Enjoy the location in your mind.

Some may call this being focused—but in reality, it is much deeper and more powerful. The power of actually *visualizing* a picture—with all of its senses (sight, sound, texture, and smells)—can make the image very real. This goes beyond fantasy: it is about creating positive goals—and creating a chance for positive outcomes.

When You Are Alone and Have a Quiet Moment, Try the Following Script

Start slowly. Relax your muscles by spending a little time on each muscle group, one at a time. As you relax your muscles, you begin imagining your favorite place on earth. It can be a favorite spot you go to alone to relax, your mother's kitchen during the holidays, or a beach where you and your fiancé spent a beautiful day. Allow the sights, sounds, and smells of this wonderful place to wash over you. This should immediately bring about a change of mood. Once you are in this relaxed state, change the focus to your wedding day. Imagine yourself walking down the aisle. You are wearing the perfect gown, all your friends and family are assembled in the aisles, you are happy, and everything is exactly as you have always imagined.

You must believe that you can create your own vision. You may want to create what are called positive affirmations to help you remain focused. Say such things as, "I am capable of creating harmony at my wedding; I will welcome everyone who wants to help."

Using Meditation to Relax

Mediation is an effective avenue to help you focus on what you believe is important. The idea of meditation is to focus your thoughts on one relaxing thing at a time, and rest your mind by diverting it from thinking about the problems causing it stress. Overall, meditation can give your body time to relax by slowing breathing; reducing blood pressure; helping muscles relax; giving the body time to eliminate anxiety; eliminating stressful thoughts; promoting clear thinking, focus, and concentration; and reducing irritability and stress headaches.

Meditation Techniques

Three common techniques are to *focus your attention on your breathing* (concentrating on your *in and out* breaths), *focus your attention on an object* (completely examining a particular object), and *focus your attention on a word* (staying away from any of the "W" words). In all three cases, it is important to keep your attention focused; if external thoughts or distractions wander in, simply be aware of them—and then let them drift out. If necessary, visualize attaching the thoughts to objects, and then move the objects out of your attention.

Focus On a Word

Pick some word that has "good" vibrations associated with it for you—a word that you associate with relaxation, comfort, or peace. It could be a word such as "serenity," "cool," "peaceful," "joy," etc. To begin, just let that word hold the center of your thoughts. As your mind wanders to more stressful thoughts, gently bring it back to that word. After a while, you may find that your mind will drift to other gentle, restful thoughts. If so, just let it wander. When it does drift to stressful thoughts, bring it back to your original word, which will bring back those calm feelings of peacefulness.

You will notice that a lot of the tension that a wedding brings about is because of the feeling that your "actual self" feels like it is getting farther and farther away from your "possible self" or selves—the person you always imagined you should be. Using mediation and visualization exercises like the ones above will empower you to see that those feelings are exactly that: feelings, only—and not reality. Visualization and meditation can be powerful tools in reconciling your actual and possible selves.

2

DEALING WITH YOUR FAMILY

War and Peace

BACKGROUND

BEING BORN TO your family was not your choice, yet, remaining part of your family *is*. In marriage, couples take wedding vows, committing through sickness and health, good times and bad, until "death do we part." Although we never formally make these vows to our family members, they assume that the same tacit vows of loyalty and love apply for them—and we, in turn, assume the same from them. We would like to believe that our families were at one time normal, and we attribute any recent "acting out" as a result of the stress, adjustments, and transitions that come with a wedding. In some way or another all families are dysfunctional—maybe like your family, where conflict and misbehavior took place on a continued basis your whole life, and you have grown up with the conception that this is normal—and for some reason or another, all the dysfunctional members of this family show up to a family occasion to remind us of what the term means. For all the years that our parents tried to keep weird Aunt Rosie hidden in the attic and Uncle Jonathan out of sight under the rug—without fail, they manage to crawl out from the woodwork and onto the dance floor on your wedding day.

Weddings are a time for families to communicate with one another and a time to understand one another's needs, goals and challenges in life. Events, particularly celebratory ones, can offer a time to heal from losses, forgive others and ourselves, and let go of the pain that comes from disappointments. The wedding can also be used to strengthen more long-standing themes: family values, traditions, our common heritage, and shared life experiences. Likewise, we can use these traditions and rituals to connect us to our past—as they provide us a window to the generations and times before us.

There are many reasons that you and other family members may feel that the nuclear family has dissolved. Family members moving away, separating, divorcing, retiring, or moving into a retirement community (not to mention the pressures that our frenetic world creates) are all forces that cause many families to be more out of touch than in earlier generations. This trend makes the linking of generations and the maintenance of traditions, like a wedding, more important than ever, as children need some way to learn about the past, establish a cultural identity, and connect to preceding generations.

As we grow older, our basic needs stay the same, while our desire to share information with those who are younger increases. By participating in traditions and rituals, both generations can have their needs met. But keep in mind that not everyone in the family may be a "willing participant" at all times: youth, in particular, are known for going through cyclical attitudinal changes. However, as you acknowledge the traditions and rituals present in both of your families, take time to also recognize the strength you gain from these traditions. They make your family unique and provide understanding, continuity, closeness, and appreciation for one another. You can start doing this today by realizing the daily things you do that make your family special; these "little things" shared together are really memories in the making. You and your fiancé can use this time to talk about the good times by sharing stories, and use this time together in cooperation and reconciliation, if needed.

As a therapist, I have witnessed the growing movement toward using the wedding as an opportunity to reconnect to family and bring generations together. However, with more and more brides and grooms emerging from blended families and stepfamilies, the wedding can present additional challenges regarding traditions, communication, and preferences: who walks the bride down the aisle, where do stepparents and former in-laws sit, etc. This section will present some common issues your family may be presenting you with lately—and some ideas on getting through them, with your sanity intact.

PRESENTING PROBLEMS

Conflict With Your Parents

Chances are, this may be the first major event in your life that you are planning (mostly) on your own, as an adult. *Even if it isn't, keep reading; there are ideas here that any bride-to-be will find helpful.* Though you have decided to shoulder much of the planning yourself, there are no doubt times that you may need your family's advice (particularly your parents'). There will also undoubtedly be times when advice is offered although it is not welcomed. The extent to which you have relied on your family before will often determine, to a large degree, how you elicit and receive their advice and involvement in your wedding planning. If you were quite independent as a child, you may be used to minimal direction; if you were (or still are) very dependent on your parents' help, most likely you will need it now as well.

Just as the dependence brides have on their parents can cover a wide territory of possibilities, equally wide is the range of conflict you may be having with them. You may feel insulted at how childish everyone is treating you; suddenly you are back in high school and being told by your parents what you should wear to the prom. Or you may be having serious arguments about deeper issues—who should or shouldn't attend the wedding, disagreements on issues between you and your siblings, even resentment from them over your choice of partner.

It is important to try to understand where this conflict is coming from. If Mom insists on constantly reminding you that you have picked the wrong florist, it's probably because she wants to be more involved in your life, or realizes that this wedding is the last thing you will do as a single person—or a hundred other reasons you can forgive her for. On the other hand, if your arguments are over something more serious, you should take the time to address them now.

FOR LESS SERIOUS CONFLICTS, TRY TO:

- **Become an Active Listener:** Active listening involves the process of listening, clarifying, giving feedback, and self-disclosing. It involves the participation of both parties in verbal and non-verbal ways. The use of "I" statements is imperative.

- **Make Eye Contact:** Be sure to look your parent in the face most of the time—especially look at her or his eyes. *(Try not to let your eyes roll too far back into your head.)*

- **Be Aware of Other Non-Verbal Signs:** Pay attention to how you place your arms, and lean forward when necessary; also notice head nodding, degree of personal space, and smiling. *(Remember they have told you for years to, "Get that grin off your face"—now is not a good time to remind them how worthwhile all the orthodontic work was.)*

- **Paraphrase the Other Person's Message:** Paraphrasing means stating in your own words what someone has just said. Use phrases like:
  - What I hear you saying is . . .
  - In other words . . .
  - So basically, how you felt was . . .
  - What happened was . . .
  - Sounds like you're feeling . . .

  Your parent will know that you have understood what she or he has said and has the chance to clarify, if necessary. *(Or he or she will ask you ten times—"Do you hear what I am telling you?" "Yes" is usually a good answer.)*

- **Ask Clarifying Questions for Better Understanding:** If something is unclear to you, ask a question to get more information. Such questions make you an active, interested listener; your parent can tell that you've been listening enough to have a question and care enough to ask—*and may wonder why you couldn't have learned this one as a teenager.*

- **Provide Appropriate Feedback:** Feedback should always be given in an honest and supportive way. This means both good and bad. (*Also, the "break it to them gently approach" should apply— since most likely they are getting older.*)

- **Empathy and Openness:** It can be difficult to be empathic if you have had different life experiences, but trying to understand how your parents might feel will help you with hearing what they are really trying to say. *Try to imagine how hard it is for them to understand why you need a three-piece live band at the wedding—when as a child your parents' families couldn't even afford a record player.* Be a supportive but neutral listener. Attempt to put yourself in the other person's shoes in terms of trying to understand how he or she feels.

Go out of your way to make your parent(s) feel that you are listening to, and really considering, their ideas. You may be pleasantly surprised to find that often, their disapproval of something you are doing is not because they necessarily want something to be a certain way; rather, they simply want to feel like a valued and respected part of the wedding (and in effect, of your new life). *Also, remember to avoid getting on Mom's bad side at all cost: in the not too distant future, you may be calling her at midnight for some tips on how to get that first screaming baby of yours to sleep.*

For some of you, however, the conflicts you are experiencing now may be more serious, or symptomatic of deeper problems in your relationship. In particular: if, as a child, you experienced some form of parental neglect (abandonment, overprotection, too much criticism, mental illness, substance abuse, etc.), you may lack some skill in taking care of your own needs. Mostly likely, you become anxious or overwhelmed in the face of adult decisions.

Try Some Self-Nurturing

Make the decision to reward yourself by doing something comforting for *you,* today. For example, if you are having one of those days where absolutely nothing seems to go right—the flowers you wanted for the reception are out of season, your college roommate just let you know that she can't attend the bridal shower, etc.—change that, right now, by nurturing yourself. Seek out a friend and find an activity that makes you feel good: see a movie, go shopping, or just take a walk and catch up on things. Choose to remember better times—actively recall things that your parents did to nurture you as a child that made you feel good. (Most likely, it was something as simple as a warm blanket and a good story, or chocolate milk and a hug.)

You can also think back to your childhood and do something you wished your parents had done when you were sad or disappointed. Remember to forgive them for what they didn't do then and can't redo now. Instead, commit to treating yourself in some special way—at least for a few hours, before you go back to worrying about the wedding.

Conflict With Your Siblings

You may notice that although you and your sibling(s) are adults, you are still great at acting precisely like children. And although as children you were very good at bossing each other around and beating each other up when called for, your nastiness to each other hurts more now.

Regardless of your birth order, now that you are the one getting married, childhood jealously and favoritism can bring up a range of emotions in your siblings, which in turn are projected onto you. You may notice little sarcastic statements like, "Now, since you are getting married, I will have to wait until mom and dad have time (or the money) to help me with . . ." etc. etc. After one or two nice comments like this, you might be tempted to counter with, "But you have always been their favorite"—which is just the beginning of an escalating conflict. Whether actually true or not, and no matter what it is that's causing your sibling to feel this way, the important thing is that they *perceive* that the emotions, finances, and time expended on you consequently decreases what your parent or parents can give to them.

EMPATHIZE, VALIDATE, ACKNOWLEDGE

Put yourself in their shoes for just a moment. (Okay, this may be hard: we know that you were *actually* the favored child.) Before you explode with defenses, calm down and think of the times that they were the center of attention and how you felt then; you will have some idea of what they may be going through now. Either way, the fact remains that you need to be sensitive and resist the impulse to tell them, "Go fight with Mom or Dad over it." Take the high road: acknowledge that the way they are feeling now is certainly understandable—but remind them that there will be many times in the future where they will be the focus of Mom and Dad's attention.

With older siblings the situation might be slightly different. In their own special way, older siblings tend to want to control your life as they have always done—by mothering you, babying you, etc. Now that you are reaching a milestone of adulthood and probably do not need (or want) this part of your relationship with them to continue, what feels like newfound independence to you may feel like rejection to them. However, for some older siblings, there may be more sensitive issues involving their own personal situations as well. The whirlwind surrounding your wedding may bring up their own fears that they may never get married, or regrets about their own looming (or recent) divorce, etc. They may just need to "vent," or worse, lash out, and your wedding plans give them the opportunity to do so.

Younger siblings, on the other hand, may feel that for the first time you are getting more attention from Mom and Dad, and their role as "the baby" is being ignored. They, in turn, may become demanding and want to be the center of attention again—taking this out on you, your parents, or both. Your parents no longer have the authority to separate the two of you and stop the fighting—they can't send you to your room or pull the car off to the side of the road. However, they can try to listen to and support each of you. If you can remind them of this wonderful ability that they still possess, you will go a long way to easing the situation with your sibling.

Use a Technique Called Reflective Listening

The next time you have the opportunity to speak with your sibling—about anything—try this exercise. Begin by initiating good eye contact, and do your best to maintain it throughout the conversation. When you do speak, try to summarize what the person is saying and repeat it back—without copying it verbatim. (*Oh, so you think that purple is the way to go for the bridal party's dresses, then?*) This signals that you are listening and value their input. (Notice I said "signals." Whether you actually are or not will be left to your discretion.)

They may clarify or expand on an idea; just keep listening without actually committing to a particular position or side. Be careful not to be overly placating or you will come off as condescending. (Remember, you have lived with this person; they know what you are up to!) When the time comes to make a final decision, and it doesn't include any of their suggestions or recommendations, you can at least say it was taken into consideration. This approach will facilitate greater involvement and fewer hurt feelings. **Perhaps the most important thing to remember is that most times, once the wedding day is here, this "issue" will probably be the last thing on their mind.**

Conflict With Your Soon-to-Be New Family

In case you haven't noticed, there is a direct correlation between the number of family members attending a wedding and the combination of potential conflicts. By now, you have undoubtedly had years of managing conflict within your own family; and by this stage in your life are probably very skilled at handling and coping with a variety of family issues. But by getting married, you have just doubled (or more, if your fiancé has divorced parents, an additional set of siblings, and perhaps some stepparents) the potential for arguments, conflicts, and disagreements.

You may have problems with his family and vice versa. Your groom may have unresolved issues with his family as well. And that says nothing about how the two families are getting along, which may be strained by the limited time there is with which to get to know each other, the stress of just planning the wedding, or many other reasons. For example, many families today come from different parts of the country or world; talking about their children's wedding can be difficult enough without a language barrier. However, the most common—and often most delicate—reason for a conflict is a culture clash of one kind or another. This may stem from a difference in geography, politics, or socioeconomic background—or a multitude of other factors. In any case, you have been raised one way (and your groom, I am sure, loves you for this), but that may cause some conflict on how you perceive, or even treat, your groom's family. A slight variation on this is that sometimes people marry into families that are almost just like their own—and here the conflict also exists in the form of competition.

Above all else, remember that this is the family who raised your fiancé—so they do have their share of good points (even if it feels like they are sometimes hard to find). Say, for example, your fiancé's family gets together every Sunday for dinner. The conversation at these dinners might drive you up a wall (sports, sitcoms—hello?), but you can, instead, choose to focus on positive sides: your fiancé comes from a family that values communication, spending time together, and little rituals.

Shift Perspective

Try not to take the "them against us" or "me versus them" attitude. Rather, just accept that these people are different from you and your family. Understanding where they have been in their own lives will give you tremendous insight into what they are saying and why they act the way that they do.

Knowing more about your groom's family can certainly help, now and in the future. But don't just learn about your fiancé's family from him, do your own investigating. Sure, go ahead and dig through the endless boxes of baby photos—but also take the time to ask his family to share stories about themselves and him. This will give you a better and bigger picture about how they parented, and who they are as people. For example, you may find their reluctance to splurge on the wedding is maddening. However, you may react differently if you take the time to learn that your fiancé was born into a poor family, and that they made great sacrifices for their children—and they still cling to some of those values today. You should want them to know about you, as well, so that they may understand how you were raised and where you are coming from. This is a learning process for everyone, so be patient! Remember, it took you sixteen years to become smarter than your own parents.

Some Things to Think About

Differences in values and beliefs can become a source of stress to intergenerational relationships. The **social norms** prevalent for you and your fiancé's generation are no doubt different than what your parents and grandparents were raised with. Disagreements over how to spend money, religious beliefs, and other values add tremendous stress to wedding planning. Differences in developmental stages of family life can be a source of stress as well: older parents may be dealing with their own aging, health issues, retirement plans, or relocation needs. Likewise, their children must accept that their parents are older and may not be able to cope as well with the stresses and changes going on as they did when they were younger.

Differences in parents' expectations for their children, and the actual children's dreams and behaviors, may also present sources of stress. The wedding you are planning, your choice of mate, the career you have chosen, or any number of lifestyle choices you live out, may not be what your parents had hoped for you. Children may have achieved all that their parents had wished for, but their relationship may lack affection, warmth, respect, open communication, and honesty. Similarly, adult children often have differences in expectations for their parents and their parents' behavior—resulting in disappointment. However, you *can* make the decision to build and maintain a healthy relationship between the generations in your family. Building and maintaining healthy intergenerational relationships can give individuals and families knowledge, respect, and appreciation for one another. Generations can learn from one another and support each other during the transitions and stresses of life.

If you find that you are facing family issues of your own as the wedding planning intensifies, address the situation. Remember to enjoy this process, your fiancé, and other aspects of your life (yes, even your family). Try to anticipate trouble spots and attempt to deal with them appropriately in a preventative way. Be aware of the signs of stress, and realize that the wedding is a rehearsal for how you two will treat each other, and others, in your new life together.

3

ISSUES WITH YOUR FRIENDS

Drama and More Drama

BACKGROUND

As you are probably recognizing now—or at least as your friends have been reminding you lately—marriage is one of those major social transitions that can have the tendency to push friendships to the side.

Now that you are engaged, everything involving your friends seems to be upside down. As you become closer with your fiancé and the wedding plans intensify, you probably have begun to notice a natural, unspoken gravitation toward your family (and his). As this happens, it is natural to decrease the time spent with your friends. (Think about it: how many more times a week or month are you calling—or seeing—your mother, father and siblings since you got engaged?) And the time that you do have left to spend with friends must now increasingly be split between his friends and yours. Adding confusion to this is the fact that while you love your fiancé to death, you may never for the life of you figure out how he has made his choices in friends. Another factor that you may not even notice is your acquaintances—remember them? While some of your closest friends are active in the wedding planning, most likely your acquaintances and intermediate friendships have probably already been muted.

What's going on here? Actually, the roles that your friends play in your life have probably been shifting for years, without you giving it much thought. Our first friendships are often as young children, with our sib-lings. As you learned to play, listen, and trust, you and your brothers and sisters shared confidences, recognition, humor, advice, and wisdom. As you grew and developed friendships of your own outside the family, these first friends often resembled your siblings in a variety of ways. And as you entered adolescence, you looked toward your friends for the support and sense of community they provided. At some point, it was common (and natural) for your friends' influence and importance to eclipse that of your family's—and you believed that these friendships would last forever. Like most of us, you have probably overlooked the subtle damage and hurt feelings this change in priorities caused your family members.

When you move away from your parents' home and begin life on your own, friendships are essential in providing an extension for the sense of belonging and community you are missing. (In some cases these friends substitute for the family or community you never had—or felt that you never had.) The bond you and your friends have is strengthened by the common challenges you face as everyone transitions together into adulthood.

But how that changes when you become engaged. Suddenly, once again, your parents and family are at the center of everything—and for more genuine reasons than that they are the ones footing a lot of the wed-ding bills. (Psychologically, when children feel insecure about any monu-mental event or transition in their lives, they have a tendency to return emotionally to a "safe place" and find security, which is traditionally with their parents.) And since the wedding is probably the biggest event that you have coordinated on your own until now, you may feel the need to seek the advice and reassurance of the adults in your life.

Don't let this reconnection with your family (particularly your par-ents) scare you. The priority we place on friends and family has been constantly in flux since our childhoods. And really, your parents won't want that much of your time with you and your new spouse. (If they are not encouraging you to go out with your friends right now, they will once you have children—so they can have plenty of time to get to know their grandchildren while babysitting!)

Knowing these shifting dynamics are normal should help defuse any regret you are feeling for temporarily leaving your friends behind.

Particularly if you are one of the first or last of your group to be married, you may feel left out from the singles' or couples' life. Remember that although the relationships are no longer the same, different can be good, and this change might only be temporary as others in your group get married over the coming months and years. Trust me: you will come around and reestablish your bonds—girls' night out or your groom's Sunday night football parties cannot survive as coed activities—before you know it. Sooner, rather than later, everyone begins getting engaged one after the other; before long, you're earning frequent flyer miles and traveling to weddings across the country together.

PRESENTING PROBLEMS

Losing a Companion

Just as you are feeling a tremendous sense of security from getting married and having a lifelong companion, you may be beginning to feel like you are losing some lasting friendships. You have your own demands on your time—not least of which is the wedding itself—and most likely your friends are themselves becoming involved in more serious relationships if not wedding plans of their own. However, as we discussed above, keep in mind that the balance between our friends and family has always been shifting at different times in our life. Although once your life settles down after the wedding you may find that you have less time for friends than you did during your college days, for example, the friendships you do have will be treasured more dearly.

An Increased Sense of Privacy Develops

In the not-too-distant past, you were able to tell your friends anything and everything about your then-boyfriend. What a difference a name makes: now that you are an engaged couple, you are probably less likely to relay the intimate details of your private life to your friends. Because, after all, you are probably confiding in your fiancé, as you should be. This can be healthy, to a point, and it goes to show the sanctity with which we (still) view marriage. But can we overdo this sense of privacy? Many brides-to-be find themselves ignoring their friends when it comes to wedding plans; simple, everyday decisions become "nobody's business." You might not even notice that your friends' feelings are getting hurt, fueling their sense that "you have changed." It is perfectly natural for *relationships* to change—just don't get so wrapped up in the wedding planning to the point where you change as a person and (unintentionally) mistreat your friends.

EMPATHIZE, VALIDATE, ACKNOWLEDGE

If a friend complains that you are snubbing her, put yourself in her shoes for just a moment. How much time have you been spending with her lately? When you do get together, do you talk about things that are important to her life—or is it all wedding, all the time? Realize that being a friend is a two-way street. Go a step further and let her know that you recognize your selfishness and will commit to being a better friend.

Alone in a Crowd

Have you woken up recently and asked, *Where am I,* or *Who have I become?* Oftentimes, once women become engaged, they quickly give up their casual friends and spend increasingly more time bonding with their fiancé's family and friends. As a result, this shift begins to strain the few deeper friendships that are maintained. If you are one of these women, you may feel as though you do not recognize yourself anymore (shopping in strange stores for things you never cared about might be a clue). Again, this might not be a "problem," and if it is, as with all the things in Occasional Therapy, sometimes simply being aware of the problem is enough.

Bad Reactions From Friends

Now that you are getting married, your friends have all been nothing but 100-percent supportive of you, displaying all those personal qualities that drew you to them in the first place—correct? Yeah, right. The wedding is a powerful force in our lives, even affecting those outside our families. See if any of your friends have been exhibiting any of these less-than-friendly qualities lately:

- Judgmental attitudes regarding your plans or decisions about your wedding
- Jealousy toward you, your fiancé, or your relationship
- Complaints—voiced or implied, about the perceived abandonment you are putting them through
- Competition—competing for your attention or the attention of mutual friends; trying to compare wedding plans, or worse, the quality of your respective relationships

Try to understand why your friends are feeling this way about you. What is going on in their lives that may be projected onto you? What needs of "theirs" might you not be meeting? What expectations of you do they have that might be unrealistic or unreasonable? Remember that you are not responsible for how anybody else feels, and most importantly, that no one can make you feel bad about yourself. That is something only you can do.

I have included some "active listening" tips below, a technique highlighted in Session One.

BECOME AN ACTIVE LISTENER

Active listening involves the process of listening, clarifying, giving feedback, and self-disclosing. It involves the participation of both parties in verbal and non-verbal ways. The use of "I" statements is imperative.

- **Make Eye Contact:** Be sure to look your friend in the face most of the time. (*Like you did when she told you about her "nightmare date."*)

- **Be Aware of Other Non-Verbal Signs:** Pay attention to your body language. (*She will pick up how uptight or interested—or disinterested—you are by just looking at you.*)

- **Paraphrase Your Friend's Message:** Paraphrasing means stating in your own words what someone has just said. Use phrases like:

  - What I hear you saying is . . .
  - In other words . . .
  - So basically, how you felt was . . .
  - What happened was . . .
  - Sounds like you're feeling . . .

Your friend will know that you have understood what she or he has said and have the chance to clarify (and ask a million more questions—as usual). (*Watch out—no further questions from a once-talkative friend could be the beginning of "the silent treatment." So encourage* **validation** *to be assured that she understands.*)

- **Ask Clarifying Questions for Better Understanding:** If something is unclear to you, ask a question to get more information. Such questions make you an active, interested listener. *After all, this is probably how you first became friends—by sharing stories, secrets, and listening to each other intently for hours and days on end.*

- **Provide Appropriate Feedback:** Feedback should always be given in an honest and supportive way. *"Yes, no, maybe" answers don't count. This is a time to say what is on your mind and move on. Most likely, if you are having a wedding conversation, you* *both want and need to* be heard. Don't spend your time thinking of what you are going to say before she has even finished talking. You can take a break, and there is nothing wrong with saying, "I need to think about that a moment."

- **Empathy and Openness:** It can be difficult to be empathic if you have had different life experiences, but trying to understand how someone might feel will help with hearing what he or she is really trying to say. *Try to imagine how hard it is for a single friend to understand why you are upset that you can't fit into your size zero wedding gown—when she is a plus size and doesn't even have a boyfriend.* Be a supportive but neutral listener. Attempt to put yourself in the other person's shoes in terms of trying to understand how he or she feels.

INSIGHTS

MAINTAINING FRIENDSHIPS MAY become a challenge as you and your groom-to-be become intensely focused on your romantic relationship, work to make room for each other's friends and family, and of course, plan that wedding. If you have friends that are exerting pressure, try to understand where this is coming from. They are most likely feeling that you are gaining "something" they may never have, particularly if they are single. Moreover, they may be worried that they are losing a valued friendship. Keep in mind that "good friendships are hard to find," and of course, they are worth cultivating. Remember to keep the lines of communication open—as you have done during your own times of need—and you will always remember exactly why they are your friends. In short, a good motto to always remember is, "Empathize. Validate. Reassure."

SPECIAL CIRCUMSTANCES

Bittersweet Moments

BACKGROUND

$\mathcal{E}$ACH FAMILY COMES to a wedding with a unique set of circumstances; some are more common than others, and some are more difficult than most. Perhaps these circumstances involve your fiancé's family, but regardless, they will become your concern if they have not already. I have attempted to address some of the more commonly occurring circumstances in this session.

PRESENTING PROBLEMS

Your Divorced Parents

The divorce of one's parents is generally one of the most painful events in life, and, like all other major life events, it may impact your wedding. If your parent's divorce occurred recently (while you were a young adult), going through the wedding process now may prove particularly difficult. Divorce often creates such a powerful sense of loss that you may be feeling like your parents are no longer available. This is especially tough, since traditionally young adults still depend on their parents to help them make the transition to independence. It may be difficult for you to accept the changes that your parent(s) are going through; for example, you may wonder how holidays and other family traditions can possibly have meaning again.

Whether the divorce was two years ago or twenty years ago, you may have some fear that the original bad feelings that brought your parents to that point will resurface on your wedding day. If one or both sets of parents have been divorced, there may be awkward situations that arise (beyond the usual tense atmosphere). If your fiancé has not experienced the divorce of his parents, it may be difficult for him to relate to your anxiety. Instead, you may find that your siblings are helpful in talking you through your fears, as they have shared in the divorce experience with you.

Oftentimes when parents are divorced, they bring baggage of their own to the wedding—arguing about who sits where, how much of the extended family to invite, which sets of parents' wishes are considered in the planning process, etc. Why is it that our parents have had their own successful lives, raised us and our siblings, and still can behave so much like children themselves? Who knows, and that may be another book entirely. But it is crucial that you treat your parents as the adults that they are (you will notice the "take the high road" advice permeating throughout the *Occasional Therapy* book series). Try to not get drawn into your parents' issues, but instead consider what is best for you in that relationship. Parents will think that they are right, just as you will at times, but as the bride you need to realize that each parent is responsible for his or her own issues.

You may notice that in some cases you are more influential or effective than your fiancé in making the peace within his family, and vice versa. Most likely you are not as emotionally involved in the ongoing dispute, which may make it easier for you to help find solutions. But keep in mind that if you work to correct things and a situation backfires down the road, your fiancé may naturally cast the blame on you. It is advisable to talk through this point with him now, before you adopt the role of peacemaker.

EMPATHIZE, VALIDATE, ACKNOWLEDGE

IF BOTH PARENTS are creating friction for you, tell them you feel that is the case, but do so on a separate, one-to-one basis. As you have probably learned from years of experience, each parent has his or her own distinct way of reacting to things.

Consider all of these things as you plan your wedding. Just as the wedding can provide a positive start to mending bad relationships, it can also point good relationships in the wrong direction. Remember that decisions regarding your own parents' and stepparents' role in the wedding planning or wedding day are decisions ultimately between you and your fiancé alone. Try to respect your fiancé's views regarding his parents, but more importantly, try to understand the reasons shaping his views. Realize that issues that are allowed to erupt at the wedding—if not resolved now—will undoubtedly follow you both into the marriage.

Unfortunately, traditional wedding etiquette is derived from thinking that was prevalent a generation—or generations—ago, and it overlooks how much divorce is a way of life in today's society. As a result, there are fewer models to rely on and less "conventional wisdom" to back you up if you have divorced parents. Many anxieties about your divorced parents stem from the expectations that things "should" be a certain way but cannot be because of the situation. Sometimes you may not even want things to be that way, but pressure from family members makes you feel that your deviation to accommodate your divorced parents will make your wedding less than perfect, more complicated, or a potential disaster!

Remember that tradition is important, but so is compromise. Making decisions just to keep the peace between mothers, fathers, or stepparents could potentially ruin your wedding day memories. Compromise is the key here. If this day is to be as much about you two as it should be, choosing everyone's place in your wedding planning and wedding is about what *you* feel. Make the decisions that feel right to you, realizing that you may be able to offer creative compromises. Don't overestimate the power of your initial, gut-level reaction to any issue that presents itself. We have the tendency to overly *intellectualize* issues and downplay our own judgment. Likewise, it is perfectly healthy to realize that everyone's role is not equal: Mom, Dad, Step-Mom, or Step-Dad have each played a different role in your life, and can each play a different role in the wedding without you feeling badly about it. Be respectful, but be truthful when you make these decisions.

When a Parent Can't Attend

As much as brides and grooms may complain about how overbearing their parents can be, the thought of not having one, or both, parents at their wedding is unthinkable. Yet for reasons beyond our control, the absence of one parent from the ceremony—due to heath issues, an extreme distance to travel, or because they have passed away, among other reasons—is possible.

Your wedding day is probably one of the most difficult days to face without a parent. You may be experiencing any number of difficult emotions: from feeling ambivalent about your future in-laws to wanting them to adopt and love you (in some way compensating for your loss), or wanting to reject them because they are *nothing* like your parents were or are, to even fearing that you may grow to love them, and then they will leave you, too. Most often, however, the sadness comes from the feeling that you have finally found *the one* and now your parent(s) are not here to share this most important moment in your life. If other circumstances (a divorce or estrangement, for example) result in your parent or parents not being at your wedding, you may feel angry: you need their help and support and they are not there for you, a feeling that may also bring with it guilt. Remember that, really, it is not their fault and know that if they could be there they would. Keeping the memory and honoring those parents who can't be with you on your wedding day, can be an uplifting show of love and family to all in attendance and does not have to dampen such a joyous occasion.

In most traditional weddings, both the bride's and the groom's family share in the responsibilities and joy of the wedding. The absence of a parent(s) often creates an uncomfortable imbalance. Because of this, the bride or groom (or occasionally, some other family member) may take a defensive role and try to protect the affected person, attempting to shield him or her from the feelings associated with the vacuum caused by the parent's absence. This action may be entirely natural, and at other times it may seem quite forced. You can still respectfully and lovingly honor the absent parent in a manner fit for this special and joyous occasion.

If both your parents are attending and one of your fiancé's parents is not, you may notice that he feels empty, sad, or even jealous of your parents' presence. As a result, you may feel guilty, which is a perfectly valid reaction. However, do not let this guilt overwhelm you; you should continue to embrace your parents. And you may be surprised to see that this, in fact, is comforting to your fiancé. Knowing that his parent(s) will be acknowledged and remembered—and that your parents will now become part of his family—will only add to the security that your union will create, and it may ease some of the pain he is feeling.

The Estranged Parents

This is admittedly a difficult situation. You have a parent to whom you haven't spoken in years, or possibly ever. Suddenly, the emotions of the wedding, the idea that you someday will have children who you will want to know their grandparent, or perhaps even pressure from a family member, may make you consider inviting—or at least contacting—this parent. That is a decision that is up to you and no one else. But be aware of the fact that once you have opened the lines of communication, you are not guaranteed your wounds will close.

Those of you operating with a "**just-world**" view—that the world is fair, and things happen for a reason—may be setting themselves up for disappointment. You must be ready to accept whatever response may follow, including a parent who may be resentful, not ready to meet you, or overly eager to become part of your life. Likewise, the parent or parents who raised you may not necessarily support or agree with your decision; after all, this marriage may open up some old wounds for them. Try (as hard as it is) to be considerate of everyone else, but ground yourself, and most importantly be true to yourself. Finding a place for your estranged parent in the wedding, even if you want to do so, can be difficult. And always remember that choosing to honor someone in your wedding celebration is just that: an honor, not an obligation.

The Ex-Partner Dilemma

For any number of reasons, one of your ex's may be in attendance—perhaps this may be a second marriage for either you or your fiancé, and there may be children involved. If it's a first marriage for you, perhaps one of you has remained friends with an ex-boyfriend or ex-girlfriend over the years and wants him or her to share in this special event. Whatever the case, the "ex-partner" issue can be delicate, or worse.

 ## Attempt Open Communication

If you are the one whose ex is involved, discuss your desire/decision to invite him or her. Focus on the reasons it is important to you, and stress to your fiancé the fact that all relationships are different and that all relationships are important—in their own way. Ask for suggestions on how you can possibly make the situation more comfortable for him. When threatened by someone not coming, evaluate how this may affect all other associated relationships before making a decision to invite or not to invite. Always keep in mind "the big picture."

If he is the one who wants an ex at the wedding, try to pause and figure things out. Rather than impulsively react or throw an ultimatum at him, first try to really hear him out about what this relationship means for him—and then let him listen to you. If he wants his ex-girlfriend in your lives, maybe a compromise would be to all go out together after the wedding when you are hopefully feeling more secure and less jealous after your big day!

Since this is a very complicated (and actually, very common) scenario, the key here is honest, open communication. Try to assess what this is really about for both of you. Listen carefully and sort out the true meanings behind you and your partner's words, and then let that guide your reactions. How would you feel if the ex-girlfriend came to the wedding? How would he feel? Now, what if she doesn't come to the wedding? Does that make whatever issues are bothering you suddenly go away?

Obviously, the relationship that should ultimately matter the most is the one between you and your spouse. You two need to discuss how involved any ex-girlfriends and ex-boyfriends are going to be in your life together. *There is no right or wrong here, you just need to come up with an agreement that works well enough for both of you.*

Concerns About . . . the Groom?

When you were "just" dating, things were different. If you are like many brides-to-be, once you become engaged and the wedding planning begins, things that you have never seen or expected suddenly appear: his mother is at the front door with a guest list, his brother has moved in and is sleeping on your couch, and college loan statements are being tossed on the kitchen table (to go along with the basketball sneakers on the living room floor, of course). All of a sudden, you are seeing a side (or sides) of your fiancé that you are not sure you can live with. It is not him, the person, you doubt; but you are not exactly convinced that you will fit in with his baggage, his friends, his family, or his world.

Also, I want to begin by acknowledging an incredibly delicate situation to talk about: it may be hard to admit, but there are those of you reading this who may, at times, be concerned about the person with whom you are planning to spend the rest of your life. The reasons can be many: something in your mindset—or actual situation—has changed, you have found something out during the engagement, or you have realized something about yourself, to mention a few of the possible causes. No matter what you are feeling now, always remember one thing: until the moment of the "I do," you don't have to, until you are ready. For whatever reason you are having these feelings, just putting your head down and plowing on with the wedding (because you are afraid of disappointing others, are convinced everything "will just work out" after the wedding, etc.) is not wise—and will have serious consequences in your future together.

Often, it is worthwhile to discuss these feelings with your fiancé. He may be having similar feelings and actually be relieved that you have had the courage to bring up the subject. Or, he may provide some insights that can alleviate your fears (or perhaps confirm them). However, always remember to ask yourself, if you are hesitant to speak about your own intimate feelings before the wedding, what kind of precedent are you setting for the marriage? If you are fearful of losing your fiancé just from merely bringing up a topic, then you must look at how secure you feel in this relationship.

Examine Your Feelings More Closely

Jot down a simple list of the reasons "why am I getting married." You don't have to—actually you shouldn't—put a lot of thought into this; just let the reasons roll off the top of your head. It will be helpful to follow this with another list of "what will happen if I don't get married." You will probably find yourself adding things like, "Mom and Dad will be disappointed." But don't stop there—follow each point through all the way to its logical conclusion. (How will they feel if you go through with the wedding and then are asking their advice on a divorce three years from now? Or a few years from that, after there are children involved?) You get the idea: it will be uncomfortable to think about these issues now, but it is better than facing their (more significant) consequences years from now.

INSIGHTS

MAJOR LIFECYCLE EVENTS are a time for families to come together—and they are a time when family members who are not present are missed the most. Whether you are missing the "perfect family" you once had (or thought you had) or the family you wished you could have had, remember that your wedding is a day to reflect for a moment on the inherently good qualities in your parents and families. More importantly, your wedding is a chance to take these qualities with you into your married life. Give credit where credit is due; remember the special people in your fiancé's life as well, and acknowledge either publicly or privately those who have helped you reach this point in your life.

5

INSIGHTS

A Dress Rehearsal for Life

PRACTICING THERAPISTS TYPICALLY keep a section in our clinical notes entitled "insights," "observations," or "additional comments." In this section, I have included some brief personal notes to you and your family. These are suggestions and ideas that I have collected after twenty-plus years of helping brides-to-be going through precisely the same things you are now.

STEP BACK FROM THE MADNESS

WHENEVER YOU FEEL overwhelmed by the wedding planning process, remember to first slow down and take a step back from whatever is causing you to feel this way. Attempt to ascertain exactly how you feel and *why* you are feeling this way. Try to make sure that you are not focusing so much attention on the external "wedding experience" that you have lost track of yourself and the reasons you are getting married in the first place.

If the planning of your wedding has already turned your childhood dream into a nightmare, you will find that your groom-to-be, parents, in-laws, family, friends, and almost anyone else involved will quickly become hostile and reactive. If your behavior is becoming unacceptable to yourself or others, sooner or later you will become isolated and feel lonely. Likewise, if you are not eating, not sleeping, and ignoring your physical health, you will not have the energy to move forward in what should be a beautiful time of your life.

It's Okay to Freak Out

What can you do when you absolutely feel yourself "freaking out?" (*Not* a clinical term, by the way.) You can try counting down, in reverse, from ten—maybe from fifty if the going gets rough—but really, who has time; there is a wedding to be planned. All kidding aside, what can you really do to calm down at those panicky, overly stressful moments? Try allowing yourself an uninterrupted thirty minutes to obsess over whatever it is that is bothering you. But only (and exactly) thirty minutes—and then you are done! If you need to, give yourself a half-hour of this "obsession time" every day. Get all the stress out at once: cry, complain to anyone who will listen, even talk out loud to yourself. Try it once, and you will probably agree the results can be cathartic.

Remember to stick to your promise. After thirty minutes you will be exhausted and not want to think about this problem again, at least until the next day. Keep in mind that if you do not put a time limit on this, your bad feelings will become a **self-fulfilling prophecy** (*that just means that in some way you will see to it that "you will feel bad"*).

Above all else, remember that your happiness in life does not depend on your wedding day alone. Sorry to say it, but a perfect wedding is absolutely no guarantee that you will have a great marriage and a wonderful life. Don't let the importance of the wedding day celebration disguise the day's real meaning: beneath all of the ceremony, planning and, yes, headaches, is a deeper, more meaningful public declaration involving all of the wonderful values, traditions, and family members that you cherish.

Finally, look at the wedding as a beginning: you and your fiancé's first "family tradition" together. Focus on what your marriage will mean to you—both of you—in the future. Remember that this will be the first of many traditions that you will be hosting together as husband and wife, daughter- and son-in-law, sister- and brother-in-law . . . but wait—we're getting ahead of ourselves here.

PART

2

Your Loved Ones

THE GROOM

With This Ring—I What?

BACKGROUND

You don't have to worry about the wedding; your fiancée is doing enough of that for both of you—correct? Seriously, I am sure that the wedding probably does have deep meaning for you, or you have would have never agreed to go through something like this. Though you are probably realizing by now that getting married has raised some issues of your own (personal feelings, commitment and family issues, and of course finances). Yet, even if you have been thinking about these things, those thoughts were probably brushed aside pretty quickly by the absolute whirlwind force with which your bride-to-be has set about turning her lifelong wedding dreams into reality. (*Totally not her fault, by the way; remember, she has been temporarily possessed by the wedding industrialists.*)

By now, you have realized what a huge influence gender roles and societal expectations play in how much men and women actually play in the planning of the wedding. While you may have paid some casual interest in most details (and perhaps some obsessive monitoring of the rapidly increasing bills), you certainly have noticed that your fiancée is receiving lots of "advice" from television, magazines, books, Web sites, family, friends—the entire "wedding industry" designed to cater to her every whim. And as you know, the wedding fantasy does not discriminate; it creeps into the subconscious of women from all cultures, races, religions, and economic strata.

Thankfully, this wedding madness will eventually subside. The best news for you? As a groom, the most important thing you can do requires very little "outside work" on your part; most often, you just need to be there, and actively listening, empathizing, encouraging, and validating is enough. The wonderful thing is that—in most cases—if you listen closely enough, you will realize that she is not looking so much for answers as just the chance to vent her feelings (*nice*—you won't have to actually take a stand on anything). However, don't forget to listen to yourself as well. Our culture has taught men to hide from sentiment and, at most, reserve it for only the rarest of private moments. Yet, if you take the time to actually listen to what your heart and mind are telling you, you will find that you can solve many issues yourself.

Feelings can be conscious or unconscious, but either way, they just don't happen one day. They are the result of many things: social conditioning, your own experiences as a child, the way you perceive or interpret events. The most important thing to know is that whatever they are—they are yours. No one else can tell you how to *feel*, or how you *should* feel. They certainly can tell you how they would like or hope you would feel—but you don't have to listen. There are simple feelings that are classified as basic emotions, or those complex feelings that are broader and involve a combination of emotions. Remember that feelings can never be right or wrong. They can be suppressed or held in, but then they will usually manifest themselves in some other emotional or physical way (depression, psychosomatic illnesses, tension, or very real illnesses such as ulcers and heart conditions).

There are many signs and symptoms that you may notice when you are experiencing **stress** and **anxiety**. These signs and symptoms fall into four categories: feelings, thoughts, behaviors, and physiology. When you are under stress, it is usual to experience one or more of the symptoms listed below.

Do the following symptoms sound anything like somebody you know?

FEELINGS

- Feeling anxious
- Feeling edgy
- Feeling nervous
- Feeling irritable
- Feeling wound up
- Feeling moody
- Feeling alarmed

THOUGHTS

- Low self-esteem
- Fear of failure
- Inability to concentrate
- Worrying about the future
- Preoccupation with thoughts and tasks

BEHAVIOR

- Stuttering and other speech difficulties
- Acting impulsively
- Startling easily
- Grinding your teeth
- Increasing smoking; use of drugs and alcohol
- Becoming accident-prone
- Losing your appetite or overeating

PHYSIOLOGY

- Perspiration or sweaty palms
- Trembling
- Dryness of throat and mouth
- Tiring easily
- Diarrhea, indigestion, or vomiting

These are common symptoms that many grooms experience, and many of their brides do as well. You see you and your bride are not so different, and you are actually responding to the same set of circumstances more similarly than you may have recognized.

Symptoms

ANXIETY

- Anxiety about making the right decision.
- Worried about or having commitment issues *(I'm not even sure about her, let alone getting married).*

STRESS

- Stressed about spending all this money on the wedding *(Will we be eating at home for the next five years; why can't we spend all this money on a nice trip somewhere instead?).*
- Feeling like there's too much to do, too little time to do it *(I do have a job . . . too, you know!).*

NERVOUS

- Nervous—even if you feel absolutely okay with getting married, if you're like most guys, you are stressed about accountability issues *(losing the freedom to stay out at night, see the guys when you want to, etc.).*

ARGUMENTS OR OTHER POOR COMMUNICATION WITH YOUR FIANCÉE

- You may be arguing, fighting or just plain avoiding each other lately. *Everything I say is "wrong" or a "bad idea"—so why is she asking me all this stuff?*

OVERWHELMED

- Feeling like there's too much to do and too little time to do it.
- Trying to juggle the balancing act—your job, wedding planning, family pressures, and more.
- Worrying about the looming financial pressures.

NOT SLEEPING

- Not sleeping frees up some time to work on your guest list, but it won't help with the tomorrow morning's 5:00 AM wake-up call.
- Feeling tired or fatigued in general.

ANXIETY

- Just plain feeling "overloaded" with things to do.

SADNESS

- Alternating between feeling up—then down—about leaving the single life behind, giving up your lifestyle, becoming monogamous.
- Scared that you're leaving behind the life you've grown to love, and that you may, finally—get ready—be growing up.

ANGER

- Where can we start? Your family is acting anything but friendly.
- No one seems to agree with any of your decisions.
- No one is asking my opinion about anything.

PRESENTING PROBLEMS

Shared Decision-Making

It is a given that brides-to-be usually care more about all those wedding details than their mates. But this difference can vary tremendously according to the level of shared decision-making that existed for the couple prior to the wedding. You should examine exactly how you make general decisions outside of the wedding, as a couple. (Who decides where you will go out to eat? Who chooses the furniture? What about that last trip you went on? You get the idea.) When it comes to one particular issue, for example, do you defer to the one who is smarter, handier, or more creative, or do you normally discuss every issue as a couple? Although the wedding day is for both of you (and your families and friends), men usually feel that becoming too involved in wedding plans is not manly. But realize that a little care here is helpful: if you don't speak up and instead decide to forever hold your peace on an issue that is bothering you, you set a precedent that will carry over into your new marriage.

Listening to Your Partner's Concerns

Try learning to listen to your partner's complaint without getting defensive. Share that concern with the other partner making statements within the following formula:

- When I notice this (whatever it is) happening . . .
- I imagine . . .
- Then I notice myself feeling . . .
- Avoid any "you make me feel" statements. Take responsibility for your feelings.
- Focus on empathically summarizing what the partner has shared.
- Think of it as listening to a best friend who is sharing

something that hurt.
- Try not to move into any defensiveness or discounting statements.
- Simply summarize what your partner has shared and ask, "Did I get you?"

Try Better Communication Methods

Trust me on this: a little "sensitivity" now means fewer headaches later.

- **Be aware of non-verbal signals:** Our body language (e.g., facial expressions, posture, eye contact) and vocal expressions (e.g., tone, volume, rhythm) all reveal a lot of information about how we are feeling—pay attention to what you are each *really* saying. *She will read into what you are saying anyway—so let her be right.*

- **Listen:** Indicate that you are paying attention by using nonverbal signals. Resist your "guy" instinct for a moment: do not interrupt when you are listening, keep an open mind, and be nonjudgmental. Let her finish!

- **Paraphrase and ask questions:** Repeat back what she's said and summarize. Ask questions to clarify statements. These techniques help you to avoid misunderstandings. Don't ask "open-ended questions;" be direct.

Talk About It

- **State your interests directly:** At times, it may provide an "easy out" to be vague, but avoiding the real issues doesn't benefit anyone in the long run.

- **Request that your fiancée state her interests directly:** Remember that conversations are a two-way street; you don't gain anything by steamrolling over her needs.

- **Avoid "personal" remarks:** When you feel threatened, you may resort to name-calling, but this just clouds the real issues and needlessly instigates bad feelings.

- **Avoid judgments:** Try to realize that this is a stressful time for your fiancée too (okay, *especially* for her) and just because you disagree on a few silly things, don't begin indicting her whole character.
- **Choose an appropriate tone of voice:** How many different ways can you tell your fiancée, "Sure, whatever you want?" You get the point here.
- **Be aware of body language:** Hint: turn off the football game, get off the couch, and sit up; at least pretend that you care.
- **Be positive and avoid negative comments:** See "avoid judgments."
- **Summarize and clarify the other person's comments:** Sometimes, the worst thing about another person's suggestion is that she's the one saying it. Get in the habit of summarizing what your fiancée is saying and putting it into your own words; you may find that it's more digestible that way.
- **Remain silent and listen:** I promise you—this won't hurt. Really!

Learn the Art of Arguing

- **Delay your reactions:** Don't jump to conclusions. Give yourself time to process what she said before you respond. Wait until you have all the information before you make assumptions.
- **Don't make generalizations:** Be specific and direct. Concentrate on one particular issue. Do not change the subject, and stick to the issue until it is resolved.
- **Use "I" statements:** This one you've got down, I'm sure. But actually, "I" statements help to express your own feelings, attitudes, and desires. Using these types of messages will avoid putting the other person on the defensive.

Making Too Many Concessions (Or, Losing an Argument Just To Get Out of It)

Have you ever lost an argument or caved in on something important to you? Men will do this, particularly with weddings, since they often just don't care as much as their fiancée. ("Pick your battles," you may tell yourself.) Or you may cave in because you just want to maintain a friendly relationship. Many times, although they may be afraid to admit it, men are just intimidated by their fiancée. And one last reason is perhaps the most cynical: rolling over on one issue may be a way to have your fiancée indebted to you for something else down the line.

There are both advantages and disadvantages, and I have included some major ones here to consider:

ADVANTAGES

- Solves the problem quickly
- Enhances your personal relationship with your fiancée
- Makes you (at least seem) fair-minded
- Shows respect for her
- Helps to maintain a harmonious environment (at least until the next crisis)

DISADVANTAGES

- Sets a negative precedent
- You will miss out on the chance to arrive at a "negotiated settlement"
- Feeling as though you have been taken advantage of
- If you're doing this just to win a favor later on, this tactic can backfire

This Is Not a "Play-Off Game"

Try not to "win" the argument by using less than desirable methods. Sure, you can win arguments by reverting to old-school, manly tactics such as **aggression**—in all of its many forms. However, in the long run, where will this "easy" victory get you? Your fiancée will begin to resent you, and so might others who learn of your actions. And, perhaps most importantly, you are increasing the chance that she'll merely do the opposite of what you want just to spite you.

Look at how you are acting now—are you using any of these tactics? If so, ask yourself, honestly, where you think they will get you and your relationship in the long run.

AVOID USING *AGGRESSIVE TACTICS* (DON'T BE SO MACHO)

- Threats
- Sabotage
- Insubordination
- Bullying
- Issuing ultimatums

AVOID USING THE *FEAR ELEMENT*

- Confrontation
- Humiliation
- Rejection
- Angering her—your interests will be discounted and nothing will be gained

**Definitely Avoid (At All Costs) *Insulting Her*

So, What *Should* We Be Talking About?

Follow the tips I just gave you, and you are well on your way to effectively talking and communicating your feelings to one another. The hardest part now is really figuring out *what* it is that *needs* to be said. One of the most difficult (and delicate) issues to discuss with your fiancée is—your family. Right?

What About My Family?

Weddings are a very tradition-bound ritual composed of many family-centered religious beliefs, traditions, expectations, and values. The planning of the wedding may be the first time these issues have emerged in your relationship with your fiancée. As your parents, her parents, and your respective families become more involved, they may very well exert pressures, including "seeing to it" that certain traditions are honored. Many grooms, fearing upsetting their bride's fantasy day, will defer to her and her family, even if this means ignoring the wishes of their own family. If your fiancée or her family is paying for the wedding, you may feel guilty about asking her to include details (say, a toast to Uncle Harry) at the request of your family. As you probably already know, being caught between the woman that you love and the parents that love you is a difficult place to be (and can make that "rock and a hard place" unbearable).

Your Family's Influence

Try looking closely at the influence your family has on you. What do they expect your involvement in the wedding to be? Are they critical of the role you are taking in the wedding—beyond their usual witty criticism that is? Or are they just critical of you or your fiancée? Try, carefully, to figure out if your parents' expectations and reactions are any different than they were before the engagement. This way you can determine if the wedding is the issue, or if *they* are the issue.

Different Background and Traditions

Unless you marry a sibling, no bride and groom will ever grow up in the same household and follow the same family rituals and traditions. Therefore, it is essential to identify what traditions are most important to each of you. Coming to terms with your differing backgrounds and traditions may well be your first lesson in creating mutual respect for your bride—and her entire family and heritage. How much influence one family or the other will have on the choice of traditions should be dealt with delicately. You *could* opt to eliminate all traditions—it will certainly reduce the number of disagreements. But this is not a wise option unless you are gung ho about creating hollow memories in the years to follow.

If you choose to just pay attention to the squeaky wheel—placating the family or partner who makes the most noise regarding a certain issue—be prepared for the possibility that this same imbalance will exist throughout the marriage. And if you are the party that volunteers to leave out your family's traditions, someone (at least) in your family *will* resent your lack of respect for your upbringing, culture, or heritage. Since you will always be their son, according to your parents, you may be capable of doing no wrong in their eyes—and they will oftentimes blame your bride for whatever transgression occurs. Do you really want your family to "blame" her because you don't want to take a stand? Experience has shown me that it is smarter and healthier for you and your fiancée to voice your concerns on these types of issues with one another first—and it sure beats having your mother confront your fiancée sometime in the future!

Additionally, it will be invaluable to set out to express these traditions and values to one another in terms of *what they mean to each of you*, not just what they are or why your parents want them as part of your wedding. If the discussion is handled calmly and sensitively, it can be an opportunity for a meaningful discussion about the traditions you will create as your own new family—not just now, for the wedding. This should be easy for you to approach—realize that this is not just a "wedding detail;" rather, it's a marriage detail.

The Wedding-Obsessed Fiancée

The girl who used to meet you for a drink after work, who snuggled next to you to watch a movie, is MIA (missing in action). In her place is a wedding-obsessed, **type-A** superwoman sitting at a table with stacks of bridal magazines, drinking water by the gallon with hopes that she can fit into her gown (see **Type A** and **Type B behavior patterns** in the Glossary). You may feel that your needs and your opinions—even your existence—are being ignored. While she is doing yoga and talking to the florist on the telephone at the same time, your fiancée needs to be reminded that you are getting married too.

Your "Problem" Friends—According to Her

Perhaps you have picked your college buddy to be the best man and she has always thought he was a jerk. But that is probably only fair, since her old roommate—who just happens to be the maid of honor—is not your favorite person either. The underlying issue is not really about who the best man or maid of honor is—but more about these people's influence on your soon-to-be wife, or husband in her case—and let's admit it, she does have a point: *what were you thinking?* Everyone (including your fiancée) has a right to include the people important to himself or herself in his or her wedding ceremony. Keep in mind that you will probably never like all of each other's friends all the time.

Commitment Issues

Society has taught men that they are the ones who will pursue a woman and be the one to propose marriage. Although you, or at least most men, may be hesitant to admit it, the pressure to make the right choice can be enormous. (Let alone the pressure that she will say "yes"!)

However, getting married can bring with it other fears, as you probably already know, which include:

- **No more "freedom"**: Men like to own their decisions and run their lives by their own rules. Choices that you simply used to take for granted—going out for a beer with your buddies, buying a big screen TV, playing golf on Saturday afternoon—suddenly have to be cleared with her first.
- **Loss of space**: Fear that his space will be feminized and fear she will be forbidding him to have any "guy stuff" at all.
- **One sex partner, forever**: You may be scared that sexual boredom can set in, and it will be followed by a total lack of desire; even the thought of not having options is terrifying to some guys.

And you may very well have some special commitment issues of your own. Take this time to jot them down here:

_____

_____

_____

_____

_____

You will at least want to keep these issues in mind as you read the rest of this session.

Some Things to Think About

Actually, we therapists call this "homework," but I know that you never would have read this far if I gave the section that title. Yet, no matter what you call this section, the following exercises should give you some easy, practical tips on ferreting out the feelings we have discussed.

Keep Some Time for Yourself

Okay, admittedly, this won't be a problem for most of you guys. But for any of you who feel that you are just getting way too involved with the wedding, let me tell you: you are not being a bad fiancé if you just need a break once in a while.

You may need different amounts of personal space than your bride-to-be, and this is perfectly natural. *Recharging yourself on your own time* will actually help you be more refreshed, energized, and "present" during your wedding preparations—oh yeah, and in the rest of your life, whatever that means these days.

Try Not to Be So Defensive All the Time

As young children, we learn to protect ourselves from emotional pain and unpleasant feelings. Early on, we are taught **defense mechanisms** to help us cope. These can take the forms listed below.

Try to recognize which defense mechanisms you are using. You may be making an unconscious effort to avoid, face, or accept the real issue that is hurtful. If others are accusing you of being in constant denial or rationalizing everything, ask yourself if there is any truth in what they are saying. Are you avoiding something painful?

- **Projection:** *(Well. It's you, not me, that is doing . . . causing, creating . . . etc. the problem.)* You've heard that before. Some call this the "blame game." Really, this behavior is a defense mechanism where people hide their own threatening impulses by placing them on other people.

- **Rationalization:** *(There is really no logical explanation according to you, that is, for why your fiancée would. . . .)* When people are not able to deal with the real reasons they are behaving in a particular way, they protect themselves by making up logical explanations for their behaviors.

- **Regression:** *(Wah! Wah! Wah! Stop whining!)* You've heard that too. "Oh, just grow up!" Have you ever said that before? When people face a situation that makes them anxious or nervous, they often protect themselves by retreating to an earlier stage of development.

- **Displacement:** *(Why would you come home from a dinner with your father and yell at your fiancée for forgetting to pick up the tickets from the travel agent? Especially if the honeymoon is not for another four weeks!)* Maybe because you are taking your anger out on someone else who is *not* the source of your feelings. This way, your negative impulses can be directed to a more acceptable or less threatening target, or your emotion to a safer outlet (like your soon-to-be wife).

- **Denial:** *(Okay, you don't want to face the fact that your brother's wife really doesn't want him to go to your Bachelor Party—and in fact you can't believe that he is listening to her and not going.)* But, you still keep letting him in on the plans, and you add his name to the "yes" column on the guest list. Denial allows you to unconsciously resolve emotional conflict and reduce anxiety by refusing to acknowledge the more unpleasant, perhaps painful reality.

SURVIVAL TECHNIQUES

Set Boundaries: Sure, do things that she wants and be happy about it. But if your weekly poker game is absolutely essential to your mental health, and you know you can't live without it, it's okay to put your foot down. This won't make you a bad husband (squandering away all your savings is another story), and in the long run, she'll probably appreciate you more for your sincerity.

Gain the Support of Peers and Friends: Find the ones who are already married. Ask an older uncle, brother-in-law, etc. They may be older, but the process doesn't really change—trust me, you'll learn a lot.

Face Your Own Depth of Pain: You may have childhood issues that are becoming painful as you get more involved in your wedding and the idea of commitment. Don't be afraid to let your mind wander back in time or know when something hurtful might be happening. (Okay, you can admit it: men do occasionally cry, and they are healthier for it.)

Become Selfish: It might be your bride's day, but this is still your life. You have to face, and live with, all the same decisions that will impact you personally, professionally, socially, and in every other way down the road.

Detach From Obsession: You can't control everything that you might like to or think that you can. Change only the things you can, and don't obsess over the rest. Letting go doesn't mean giving up.

Deal With Anger: It is natural to be angry, and natural not to know how to deal with it. Recognize who and what you are angry about. Express your anger in a constructive way.

INSIGHTS

MOST MEN DO not obsess over the wedding because they are, well, men, and they most likely *are* worried about things like this huge commitment they are making and the equally large amount of money they may be spending. If you are like most guys, one dream of yours was to meet a beautiful woman, make her your wife, and live happily ever after; notice that standing up on the altar in a fabulously tailored tuxedo was not in that fantasy.

Even though the wedding is really all about her, as you try to understand your bride, you can seize this opportunity to begin learning a little bit about yourself. Doing so will help make the wedding be more memorable for you, her, and each other's families. Recognize that the wedding is more than a party. Instead, it is a celebration of something wonderful—and lifelong. Yes, most of the wedding mania is geared toward her. *Just make sure that you do your best to make the marriage be about both of you.*

7

THE PARENTS

Welcome to the Family

BACKGROUND

$\mathcal{Y}$OU'VE WATCHED THE scenes play out in movies and television commercials—the images are burned into your mind: a mother and daughter smiling and laughing as they browse through floral arrangements, a father in a slight depression because his baby is getting married, a mother and son sharing that wonderful moment where she passes him the family ring to give to his beloved. And now, when it's time for your own daughter or son to finally tie the knot, you find the Hollywood script you watched over and over again is much more suited for a reality television show. Every parent reacts differently to the news of the "engagement." Some parents are speed-dialing the caterer and a photographer and calling everyone else who will listen to the good news, while other parents—who just may be less than enthusiastic—are slower to react and remain momentarily in shock, or even denial.

Many preexisting factors play a role in how you will react to the news. How long have the children known each other? (An announcement one month after the first date may elicit more shock than joy, of course.) Is the timing right for you? (If you have just entered menopause, those hot flashes might get worse before they get better.) Is the timing right for your child? Well, really—do you think, *Is it the right time for him or her to get married?*—is the better question?

So, what's *really going on* here—is this normal?

The answer is yes, and it happens a lot more often than you think. Actually, there are probably many different emotions working here. Read on to see if any of the following "symptoms" apply to you or your own spouse.

Symptoms

STRESSED

- So much to do, and so little time to take care of all the wedding planning and details.
- Stressed with your engaged child or aggravated with your other children who aren't helping enough or who just aren't getting along.
- Suddenly, your own daily routine seems overwhelming.

TIRED

- Tired, both emotionally and physically.
- Feeling that you are not as young as you once were.
- The repeated thought that it seems like only yesterday that you were changing his or her diapers, and you feel that time is passing too quickly—and this really makes you wonder how much time you have left.

IRRITABLE

- With your spouse (or former spouse) or children over wedding details.
- Even (more often than we may like to admit) over the choice of whom he or she is marrying.

■ Arguing with your child about why he or she is choosing to get married at all.

ANGRY

■ Feeling incensed about being excluded from the wedding planning.
■ Overburdened with the wedding planning.
■ Or perhaps you're getting the distinct feeling that they are just humoring you.

LONELY

■ The fear (imagined or to some extent real) that you are no longer needed.
■ The actual loss of love, attention, and time that comes with abandonment.

WORTHLESSNESS

■ Feeling under-appreciated.
■ The sense that your child is now becoming an adult and may not value or respect your decisions.

PRESENTING PROBLEMS

Changing Roles

Parenthood, as you know, changes suddenly when you make the jump from being Mom or Dad to being the mother-in-law or father-in-law. No matter how long you may have been prepared for the engagement, your new role can quickly bring about deep feelings that are tied to a whole host of unresolved issues and emotions. It is important to understand that these feelings didn't develop in a vacuum. Ongoing issues with your other children, your husband (or wife), ex-husband/wife, and issues from your own personal life become more pronounced as the "wedding" becomes one more thing to worry about.

Most children marry at about the same time as their parents are beginning to take on new and changing roles themselves. Retirement, taking care of their own parents, and the empty nest all seem to come at the same time. These changes are all normal, but underneath it all may signify an incredible loss: your own parents are entering their final stages of life, your career may be nearing its end, you may be downsizing your home, your eyesight is going—and now you are losing your baby to a "stranger."

Embrace Change

Recognize that letting go is a natural part of life. Consider your own life and how many changes you went through over the years. Going away to college, moving into your first apartment, starting your first job, having your own children, and spending less time with your own parents—these were all phases that you navigated with success while still maintaining ties with your loved ones. Recognize that your child, too, has to move on—and that in many ways, the more his or her life changes, the fonder your place in their heart will be. In fact, you should be proud that your child is taking this great step forward, a step that truly can be a tremendous move forward in his or her **self-actualization**.

Recognition of Your Own Aging

The first question most parents (okay, mainly mothers) ask themselves is, "Am I really old enough to have married children?" The answer they always seem to give themselves is, "Certainly not!" No matter what, many of us always seem to remain (in our minds anyway) about twenty-something years old. Honestly, though, this is a common way of thinking and generally isn't indicative of any serious mental disorder. In fact, it is just a normal coping mechanism, a sort of denial to deal with the fact that we, as parents, are getting older, and so are our children.

However, I do understand that it may be extremely difficult for parents like yourself to "let go" of your children and permit them become individuals separate from you (a process called **individuation**). Remember, too, that your child has enough stressors affecting him or her already. It is good to recognize and address your problems; but it's not as responsible for you to call your issues to everyone's attention at this time where—no matter how grown up and independent he or she is—your child still very much needs you.

It is imperative that you slow down, and—as in the "Changing Roles" section above—look back at your own life. Moving on is part of the natural progression of things; this isn't something that you haven't handled many times before, and with success.

Sadness Over Your Child's New Autonomy

Many years ago, when your daughter went to kindergarten for her first day of school, the excitement of that day was mixed with the sadness that came with realizing you were no longer her entire world. Yet, the deeper, underlying psychological issue was that you were realizing you were no longer in control of her whole world. Aside from moving away for college, your child's wedding is the most important milestone in autonomy. Even though your daughter hasn't lived at home for years (most likely), knowing that she is getting married, you are probably feeling that she is finally on her own.

Shift Perspective

If this is all too much for you, think for a moment about one of the possible alternatives: how would feel if your child called nightly crying that she was lonely, had no one to share her life with, and was ready to start a family but couldn't? Or imagine offering your child the chance to move back home with you and share in your new "midlife" crisis. Is the thought of having her home for dinner every night or doing her laundry and cleaning her room all over again attractive to you?

Perhaps you can see through this shift in perspective just how healthy—and necessary—her new autonomy is. Be thankful for it, and let your child share this same joy (*and do their own laundry*).

Or This:

Start collecting ideas and making lists of all the things you wanted to do—but never did—when your nest was first empty: taking a vacation, signing up for a college class, waking up at noon everyday for a week—anything is fair game. Your child's moving out to attend college is one thing, but now that he is on his own, your options are almost limitless. *Enjoy.*

MORE THINGS TO WORRY ABOUT

Meeting the In-Laws

This doesn't get any easier with age, does it? You've obviously made it this far. You have raised your own wonderful family; most likely had your own successful career, and your children certainly look up to you. But why are you still overly self-conscious or feel like you don't know how to act when meeting these people who will become part of your family forever? Meeting the in-laws for the first time and being comfortable around them afterward carries its own distinct stress. No matter what the differences are between your family and theirs—and we know that they can feel limitless—remind yourself that they (and your opinion of them) are not the issue here. As parents, I am certain that you both want the best for your children's happiness. *So you see, as in-laws you already have a common bond and mutual goals. Help foster your children's new lives together and receive the joy of watching them create a family of their own. (Yes, this means grandchildren for you.)*

Doubts Over the Bride or Groom

Is this the "right" one for my baby?

As parents, especially as mothers, we seem to have a crystal ball that tells us, and us alone, what is dangerous for our children. But for some reason, children don't want to listen to what their mothers have learned from years of gazing into clear glass (*nor do they what to hear what their parents have learned in fifty-plus years of life*). It is natural that each generation wants to make its own decisions, mistakes and all. Your parents probably felt the same way—after all, you lived and learned—and so will your children. You can only make them aware of a mistake they *may* be making—but you can't stop them from making them.

If you are doubting your child's choice of future spouse, think about whether it is the *"getting married"* part or the *"who they are marrying"* part that is disturbing to you. Even if you are consciously trying to hide your feelings from your child, unconscious actions and remarks just may make your feelings known. (*Remember how they always knew just how mad you were—without you ever saying a word. That raised brow, scary eye, or silent nod was enough to get your point across. You can't hide much from them now either.*) But try—this is going to be your new son, so give him a chance before giving him the evil eye.

And another note to moms and dads: be positive—you just might find that this new addition to your family will be the best thing that has ever happened to your son or daughter—and maybe to you, and that you have made a mistake by jumping the gun!

Identifying With Yourself at This Stage of Life

Major life events like weddings always bring us back to our own youth. Mothers and fathers seem to believe that they were never as foolish, selfish, or silly as their own children are being now; but they were certainly just as "in love" as their children are "now" as they are preparing for marriage. Yet, if your children were to ask their grandparents (your parents), they'll get the real truth: you were just as foolish, selfish, and silly at this stage of your life (and yes, probably just as in love).

Talk Openly With Your Children

Discuss this time of your life with your children, but be honest with them and yourself. You must have made at least one mistake at your own wedding—right? (If the mistake happens to be marrying your children's mother or father, you should probably select another example.) By sharing some of your own missteps with your children, you are giving "emotional permission" for them to make mistakes and are helping them overcome their struggle for perfection. However, if as a young bride or groom, you struggled with wedding issues, parental disapproval, finances, or an eventual failed marriage, you may unconsciously try to protect your children by encouraging different actions, or you may be overly critical or cynical as your own negative feelings resurface. Seeing your children walk down the same path you did can be frustrating and painful. Remember that you can only lead your children to your preferred pink champagne: you can't make them order it.

REEXAMINE YOUR OWN WEDDING EXPERIENCE

DON'T JUST RELY on your memory. Instead, take the time to actually look through your own photo album, or better yet, talk to a relative who was at the wedding. Try to do this with your child. You might be surprised to find out that your wedding reality was slightly different than the version you've chosen to remember over the years.

Confusion About Your Role After Marriage

Will I, your parent, the one who spent twenty-something years of sacrifice raising you, be welcome in your new life together after the marriage?

This is a question few parents ask their children directly, but it is the one most parents worry about—and whose answer they fear the most. From what you have seen so far, it doesn't look good: you have been asked to return the spare key to the apartment, and now you feel locked out of his or her life as well.

Remember that the foundations of trust in your relationship were laid long before the new bride or groom ever arrived on the scene. Be cognizant of the fact that the way you are feeling now is in fact due to changes in their levels of maturity and dependency, and nothing to do with love. Also, you will be happy to know that in many families, parents and children become more involved in each other's lives after the marriage. This is particularly true when both the bride and groom already have a strong sense of family and expect this same involvement as they grow. In marriages where neither the bride or groom come from strong family-centered backgrounds, they may either shy away from family involvement or, conversely, seek to create the family life they never had (which is the more preferred outcome, of course). In either case, looking at the expectations and values that you brought your child up with is a good predictor of your role in the couple's future life.

Take the Time to Plan Future Activities

Try to do some preplanning with the couple regarding the arrangement of family holidays in the future. This will help make you feel more secure that you will have a "place," and it will help to avoid some serious conflicts when the holidays do roll around.

Conflict With Family Members

Let's face it, you have known your family members a lot longer than your children have, and neither of you actually had the opportunity to choose them to be your relatives. However, the fact remains that relatives will still be at the wedding and can potentially add extra stress to both you and the marrying couple. It is important to understand that sometimes the children's resistance to invite certain (or any) relatives may be financial; other times they simply don't want strangers at their party. Trying to explain to them that "these" people are not strangers is difficult. (You can start by understanding that to them, you as parents are looking stranger and stranger by the moment.)

Try seeing it this way: since a wedding is the blending of two different families, almost half of everyone there will be a stranger to the bride and groom—so why not a few more? Truth is, it is really the selection process that troubles most brides and grooms. One might love his/her Uncle Stanley, but for years the other has despised him. Then what? Besides eloping or having the wedding on Mount Fuji, there are easier solutions.

Actually, this round of family conflict provides a way for you teach your children a valuable lesson in forgiveness. Undoubtedly, there is something every parent looks back on and wishes he or she had done differently: a hurtful remark, an insensitive or indifferent response, etc. Take the time to recognize one—or a few—of these, and go out of your way to apologize for any bad judgment on your part.

Your Role as Peacemaker

Like you don't have enough to do with the wedding right around the corner, and now you've been given another job—peacemaker. After all the years you have spent stopping the kids—the siblings, the cousins, and the neighbor's children—from fighting, you are probably pretty good at it. And everyone knows that is what parents do. However, at this stage of life, you might be in a position where making your own peace with a relative or friend before your child's wedding would be appreciated and a gift that would always be remembered.

When the Relationship Is Very Strained: Reconciling With Others

Before closing the door on a relationship, try to see how reconciliation might benefit you and your children at some point in the future. Any attempt at reconciliation can make a huge impression on our children, as they learn more from observing us more than from anything we tell them. If we teach them to become loving, respectful, accepting people, and we don't behave that way ourselves, our words will fall on deaf ears.

Attempt Reconciliation

- **Attempt deep transformation:** The past hurts are resolved, and both people heal, change, and experience closeness and satisfaction in the new relationship. This is the most desirable outcome, yet it is often the hardest to attain.

- **Shift your perspective:** You no longer expect that the other person will change. This takes an understanding of where the other person has come from, as well as how his or her behavior evolved and why. If you can (and want to) do this, you will be able to reestablish the relationship regardless of whether the other person changes.

- **Agree to disagree:** Accept that both you and the other party have never agreed on the subject matter and will probably never agree. By doing this, you will "force" both sides to develop and concentrate on other areas of the relationship.

- **Find resolution:** This is the "worst case" scenario. Resolve yourself to the fact that no viable relationship can exist. Know that you have made your best effort and that you have exhausted all reasonable approaches. This approach should be reserved only for those situations where the cause is too horrific or severe to deal with.

THE "REAL PEACE" COMES FROM WITHIN YOU

1. Eliminate irrational beliefs and distorted thinking.

2. Communicate—then mediate or negotiate.

3. Visualize your future in a positive way.

4. Remember this is not a war—but be prepared to choose your battles wisely.

5. Make peace with others, and most importantly with yourself.

6. Be honest. Come to terms with your mistakes and misgivings. Fear, self-doubts, blame, and guilt keep us from understanding others and changing our behavior.

7. Communicate. Listen to and try to understand the other person's experience. Share your own expectations, hopes, feeling, and concerns.

8. Validate feelings and beliefs. Recognize that the feelings and beliefs of adult children and their parents are real. Each deserves the right to his or her own opinions, even if those opinions are different.

9. Respect one another. Respect promotes respect and recognizes individuality. Let go; recognize that each generation makes decisions and must suffer or enjoy the consequences; allow each generation the opportunity to learn from each situation.

INSIGHTS

IT IS COMMON to feel a sense of loss as you prepare to "give away" your son or daughter; mixed emotions of joy, doubt, and fear are natural, especially if this is your first time. If this isn't your first wedding, don't try to compare their weddings and relationships, and don't anticipate having the same relationships as you have with your other children and in-laws. Most likely they weren't the same as kids, so they certainly won't be now in marriage.

Share some experiences from your own wedding and marriage with your child. It will be an opportunity for you to gently teach him or her what you have learned, and it will be a great opportunity for him or her to better understand you as an adult (and how you got to be the way you are). Always remember that it is natural for you to see your own behavior in your child's behavior.

As parents, the greatest compliment you can receive is the witnessing of family traditions passed down; but don't get hurt or offended if some are left out of the wedding ceremony. Just as you had hoped that your son would have his father's eyes or his mother's nose, his new identity in a couple will also be a unique mixture of the "best of both."

All families celebrate holidays or rites of passage that arise from their religious, cultural, or ethnic origins. Similarly, all families practice *traditions* that symbolically represent their families and connect them to previous generations. At the wedding, parents will "give away" the bride to the groom, symbolizing their "letting go" of the daughter. The children have now achieved independence, and the wedding marks the beginning of a new nuclear family; the parents' relationship with their children changes as a result. The diversity of beliefs, customs, and values in the world tend to confuse young people as they move from childhood to adulthood. They often experience considerable conflict within themselves as they attempt to internalize their own belief system. You will help them tremendously if you offer a listening, nonjudgmental ear.

Always remember that the wedding planning has barely begun, the parents haven't even checked into the hotel, and the baggage has somehow accumulated. Do your part and try to travel light.

8

THE SIBLINGS

Rivalry Returns

~

BACKGROUND

*F*OR MOST OF you, your sibling was your first friend and probably one of the best you have ever had; for many of you, this is probably still the case today. If the two of you are close in age, you have been friends—and a part of each other's everyday lives—since before you can remember. If there is a larger age difference, you most likely can still remember with fond memories the first day your parents bought him or her home from the hospital. As you grew up, you shared in all the joys and tribulations of childhood: from your first day of school to that first crush, to your teenage years and that first breakup that you thought you'd never get through, your sibling was there for you. So now that your sister (or brother) is getting married all these years later, you, of course, are happy for her (or him). Actually, maybe not.

It may be good to hear that you're not alone. If you are like most siblings, the wedding may be stirring up some mixed emotions of your own. Although for so long you shared stories about the dating game, critiqued each other's boyfriends or girlfriends, etc., now that this is the real thing, it can be scary even for you.

Your sibling's marriage can be causing confusion, stress, or even sadness for you. There may be changes in your relationship because of the engagement, or perhaps you feel that your parents are treating her differently now. Or the wedding may be unearthing deeper personal issues that you have been ignoring for a long time. Whatever the particulars of your situation, one thing is for sure: sibling relationships shape how people feel about themselves (as individuals and as respected members of a larger social group, the family). When one sibling's life changes so dramatically, it is inevitable that the other feels it as well. Even though you are both well-adjusted adults, this is certainly as true today as when you were school kids.

See if any of the following symptoms describe you lately.

Symptoms

UNEXPECTED FEELINGS ABOUT YOUR SIBLING'S CHOICE OF MATE

- Feeling sad, angry—or just perplexed—about your sibling's choice of my future brother- or sister-in-law.
- Thinking they will have a more important place in the family or will just be treated better than me.

FEELING EMOTIONALLY HURT

- By the perceived "disloyalty" as the bride/groom "chooses" to accommodate others' feelings and wishes over yours.
- That your sibling's opinion of you will change because of what your new brother- or sister-in-law says or feels about you.

JEALOUSY

- About all the attention family, parents, and friends are focusing on the wedding.
- Wishing it was your wedding maybe.
- Thinking your sibling's wedding (or marriage) will be better, fancier, or more important than yours was or ever will be.

FEELING IGNORED

- Feel the bride (or groom) is ignoring you, that you're losing your "best friend."
- Your parents may be ignoring you too.

BEING CRITICAL OF YOURSELF

- Longstanding issues of childhood favoritism or other inadequacies bubble to the surface.
- Feelings of failure, underachievement, etc., regarding your present situation, especially when compared to your sibling's moving forward with his/her life.

FEAR OF BEING ALONE

- Feeling that you are "missing out," relegated to being a spectator.
- Becoming worried that you yourself may not get married for whatever reason.
- Insecurity regarding your future role in the brother/sister's new life.

FOR OLDER SIBLINGS

- Might feel as if your wisdom and experience are being ignored.
- May feel inadequate and/or resentful, particularly if you have had or are going through a divorce, rocky marriage, or have had problems with dating and relationships in general.

PRESENTING PROBLEMS

Loss of the "Original" Family

When a sibling gets married, other siblings often feel like the family they grew up with is dissolving to some degree. When the news first hits that brother/sister is getting married, you may even feel sad or depressed. (Even if there were times you had wished that you were born into another family, it was usually because you were hoping for new parents—not for more siblings!) This tendency most likely harkens back to a very primal tendency we all exhibit in our early years: we wish that we are an only child—and can receive 100 percent of our parents' attention all of the time.

These feelings are perfectly normal. Weddings often bring back an "updated" version of those childhood feelings, as siblings feel a sense of loss and worry that nothing in the family will ever be the same again: reunions, visits, and the holidays must be shared with "an outsider"— and that person's respective family. Really, though, there is a positive side: a potential teammate for those times when you need to gang up on your sibling.

Disapproval of Sibling's Choice of Mate

So your brother or sister decides to get married, and perhaps has even found Mister or Miss Right. This should be one of the happiest times in their life, and you are already making snide comments to your parents (or anyone who will listen). Up until now, you've trusted, admired, and respected most—if not all—of your sibling's decisions, so what is going on here?

You should pause here and understand that a lot of what you are feeling is a result of the shock of being confronted with a major life event. (Even if they have been dating since kindergarten, or if it feels like they've been dating since kindergarten.) Perhaps you feel that your loyal bind has snapped, and you are now forever behind your sibling's spouse in order of importance. Additionally, most siblings believe that they know each other better than anyone else knows them; your sibling's going against your better judgment and marrying someone you disapprove of is a direct insult.

Why are you acting like this? Perhaps your sibling has a history of abandoning the family for his or her past loves, and you're worried that this will happen now to the nth degree. Of course, something called **reconstructive memory** can distort all our memories—so in any recollection with this much significance, try hard to stick to "the facts." (If you find yourself, for example, remembering that one year your brother's girlfriend convinced him not to go to your birthday party but to go surfing instead, think about whether that could have really happened, since you know your brother was only ten at the time and still doesn't know how to swim. You can discern that this incident probably never happened.)

> **Try to figure out** if you are truly unhappy with the person your sibling is marrying, or whether you are just unhappy with the fact that he or she is getting married—and the changes in your relationship that this implies. I agree with you that your relationship may never be the same, but a healthier way to look at it is that it will be different—not necessarily better or worse. If there is no common ground on which you can establish a relationship with your future sister- or brother-in-law, then you should attempt to maintain a separate relationship with your sibling. This is often a challenge, but when achieved it can lead to acceptance, and in some cases, a change in feelings toward the spouse.

Perhaps the thing that will help you most is to understand that your sibling is probably going through many of the same things you are. By getting married, she may also be gaining a sister- or brother-in-law that she didn't choose, either—not to mention a mother- and father-in-law, plus a complete new family. Try to realize how much her situation is changing, too, and put yourself in her shoes before rushing to judgment.

Think Back and Try To Remember

Think back to when you were children and see if you can remember some of your sibling's old boyfriends or girlfriends. Consider all the reasons why you disliked them. (*Go ahead. Even make a list.*) Now, was it because of some basic flaw in their personality, or was it more about how they acted or interfered in your relationship with your sibling? Do you recognize any patterns in your (or your sibling's) behavior? If there are, you should take the time now to look at those patterns.

Competition for Parents' Attention, Acceptance, and Approval

When your sibling announces his marriage plans, particularly if he is the first in the family to do so, the news can be frightening for everyone involved. Even if your relationship with your sibling remains strong throughout the wedding planning process, conflicts and bad feelings between other family members (parents or grandparents, for example) may affect your relationship.

Additionally, all children believe that their parents have a favorite child. Throughout literature and across cultures and ages, there are references to how birth order shapes our personalities. Older siblings somehow are better equipped at handling new situations (like a wedding) because they have always been "first" to do everything. (Never mind that if you ask your older sibling, they will probably tell you that they feel as if they were the experiment and you were the perfected product after years of your parents' practice.) And with being the older sibling can come great pressure to "set the standard." If you are the younger sibling, you might feel that you are expected to follow in the footsteps of the older sibling(s), and that their wedding and marriage will become the family's standard. If you are older, perhaps you will feel additional pain in imagining that you somehow let your parents down by not being the first to get married. Whatever the case, remind yourself that you are unique, and you do things for yourself—and this is also the case for your sibling, who is committing to a married life.

INSIGHTS

WEDDINGS ARE A time of tremendous change for the entire family—even for you. You are probably experiencing a real sense of loss and separation, because, after all, your sibling has openly invited a "stranger" into a private club that you have had since birth. Depending on the amount of involvement that the marrying couple is allowing or encouraging in the wedding process, it might be easy for you to feel that your opinions and ideas no longer matter. (After all, it was you they hid under the covers when you were scared as child, sneaked into the house past curfew, protected from bullies on the school bus, made holiday cards with each year, and comforted at family funerals.) Do know, however, that whatever you are feeling now after a lifetime of shared experiences together—and this sudden, imposed **adjustment** you must deal with—is valid.

Hopefully, your sibling is being sensitive to the feelings that the wedding is stirring up for you. If she is not, ask her to consider you: just because she is getting married, it doesn't mean that she loves you any less. You don't need me to tell you that although she is getting married—and is the one everyone is fussing about—you have feelings, too. Also, use this time to reflect on your own life and grow—particularly if you are dealing with marriage or commitment issues. If you are not married and would like to be, have gone through your own marital problems, are having problems with your family, or have a longstanding issue with your sibling that has nothing to do with the wedding—pay special attention to that issue as well. Try not to take out any resentment out on your sibling during what can truly be a great time for the entire family, yourself included.

3

The Couple

9

A JOINT SESSION

So Happy Together

BACKGROUND

WHEN YOU FALL in love and decide to get married, everything should be happily ever after. Sure. Too bad you can't bypass all this wedding planning or start your "ever after" about six months before the actual wedding. Before your engagement, everyone at least appeared to be normal (and yes, I realize "normal" is a relative term when talking about families). However, these days you are being hit with unexpected stresses from all over the place. Now that you are getting married—suddenly—everyone seems to become critical of everything, has a new pet issue, or is being otherwise difficult; everyone has an opinion or is creating havoc at the worst possible moment. You are already dealing with your own nerves, doubts, indecisions and the pressures that come with preparing for one of the biggest moments in your life. Now everyone wants to misbehave?

It would be nice to pretend that these issues surfacing (whether from you—the marrying couple—or your parents, siblings, friends or relatives) derive from the pressures that the modern day wedding involves. However, these problems—which typically include differing opinions on family involvement, finances, event details and more—are actually more often indicators of underlying, hidden issues that need to be worked out. The last thing I would want to do before your wedding is to add additional stress to your lives. With that in mind, I have created this section with the goal of being fun, easy-to-use, and collaborative. If you recognize the issues facing you now are ones that can be navigated easily enough with level-headedness, calmness, love, and a sharing spirit, you will overcome these issues and any others in the future.

Symptoms

NERVOUS ANXIETY

- Worried that you are making the right decisions.
- Will it ever be "normal" again after the wedding.

AFRAID

- Things will never be the same again with family and friends.
- Concerned that something will go wrong with the wedding or the relationship.

STRESSED

- Uneasy, anxious, or stressed about time, money, and each other.
- About making this huge commitment.

FEELINGS OF INSECURITY

- Insecure with one another.
- The irrational fear of rejection or abandonment.
- Feelings that the wedding won't be everything you both dreamed of.

PRESSURED

- Feeling pressure over issues with fiancé's family.
- Too many demands on your time, finances, person, etc.

PRESENTING PROBLEMS

Arguments and Other Family Disputes

As you become more enmeshed in the wedding planning process, focus often shifts from *what you want to achieve* to *doing what is right*, expected, or desired by others. The responsibility to resolve this problem is now yours as a couple. This can potentially create conflict in your relationship, as each one of you may have a different perspective and method for problem solving.

Most fights are symbolic of a larger issue. If you two (or your family or friends) are fighting all the time, it is necessary to help find resolution so that your wedding day can reach its potential. Of more importance, however, is setting the right tone for the beginning of your new life together: issues between yourself as a couple and your families most likely are linked to unsettled issues that existed before the engagement, and—like your new in-laws—will not go away when the wedding is over.

In our throwaway society, the desire to toss out something or replace it when it's broken has the potential to be dangerous to families. Why work on cultivating a relationship, when it's easier to ignore the person, or at least the real issues? There is value in taking the time to tend to and mend relationships, but it takes desire, energy and sometimes, hard work. As generations of family members become increasingly separated geographically, keeping in touch is difficult enough, even in healthy relationships. When there is trouble in a relationship, the distances grow figuratively as well. The worst thing is that the children—your children—will grow up physically and emotionally distanced from their families and find it difficult to pass down their heritage and cultural traditions—a fact that will be compounded for their kids. Theorists talk about the importance of "belonging" and attachment in developing security and healthy, intimate relationships. This sense of belonging comes first from being a part of a "family."

Conflict occurs as a result of clashing attitudes, beliefs, needs, and desires (all of which will occur—if not between you two, certainly between family members). When faced with conflict, especially in intimate family or personal relationships, people usually respond with anger or hostility, or may just become **passive-aggressive**. By practicing conflict resolution and through assertive communication you can decrease hurt feelings, add clarity to decisions, and improve your confidence in the decisions you are about to make.

Listen to Ascertain the True Issues

- Emotional versus factual

RESPOND APPROPRIATELY:
- Encouragement versus confrontation
- Restatement of opposing positions for clarity
- Finding areas of agreement
- The importance of detail to define all issues

CREATE SOLUTIONS:
- Prioritize the issues for both sides
- Identify the difficult issues
- Start with the easy issues
- Determine concessions that can be made by both parties

Stop That Fighting Now! Develop Conflict Resolution Skills

- Be specific in stating what you believe the problem is.
- Ask for feedback on the major points from your mate—don't go into this with blinders on.
- Confine your remarks and comments to only one point at a time—come with a list if you have to.
- Always consider a compromise.
- Speak only for yourself; there is no "we" in this discussion.
- Think before you speak.
- Express your feelings at a "feeling" level. Talking about the practicality of details or plans, for example, can mask how and why you really feel the way you do.

Ineffective communication or aggressive communication can be seen as controlling or overpowering. The following are some *obstacles to avoid*:

- **Directing, ordering or commanding:** These produce feelings of resentment and anger and more often than not, cause the other person to respond with hostility.
- **Warning, admonishing, or threatening:** Each indicates little or no respect for the other person.
- **Preaching or giving ultimatums:** They cause people to defend their own position even more strongly (whether right or wrong).
- **Judging, criticizing, disagreeing or blaming:** They can make the other person feel stupid, inferior, or unworthy.
- **Name-calling, other ridiculing or shaming:** These messages can have devastating effects on self-esteem.
- **Withdrawing or humoring:** Putting people off indicates we are not concerned about their feelings or mental wellness.
- **Talking about the past, because the problem exists now:** Deal with it in the present.
- **Overloading the other person:** With associated mistakes and grievances.
- **Correcting how someone else feels:** Always validate and acknowledge his or her feelings—those feelings are just as valuable as yours.
- **Trying to be the "winner":** A good compromise is always a win-win situation.
- **Complaining and whining:** It is so easy to slip into that childhood voice.
- **Sarcasm and intolerance:** This creates intimidation and blocks communication.
- **Assuming that you know why the other person is responding the way he or she is:** You are not a mind reader; just ask the reason.

SOME THINGS TO THINK ABOUT

OKAY, SO HERE it is: the homework section. I know that you barely have time lately to sleep, spend any quality time together, or get in a half hour at the gym. With that in mind, here are some guidelines that can help you get through the wedding planning better, resolve some issues before the wedding—and the nicest part—spend some quality time together again.

Unsolicited Help and Advice

People want to contribute to the wedding planning because they love you and have the desire to help you—and also because they want to feel that they are a valued part of this occasion and of your lives. Share your plans with them and encourage them to help. Giving the important people in your life the chance to be involved in planning and participating in your wedding ceremony can be rewarding for them and yes, even you. (Really!)

If you are uncomfortable about involving someone in a particular aspect, try to divert his or her attention to another responsibility that is more appropriate for that individual. Try not to shut him or her out completely—you will be sending the signal that he or she might be dismissed from your new life altogether. This can become especially challenging when you realize that while every task may be important, some aren't as "glamorous" as others (for example, accompanying the bride-to-be to her gown fitting versus putting the stamps on invitation envelopes).

Setting Mutual Goals

Saying that you and your fiancée have some decisions to make together is an understatement. The two of you should carefully discuss which decisions need to be made jointly, at the beginning of your engagement if possible. It would also be helpful to decide early in the wedding planning process exactly which issues will be negotiable and which will not. Obviously, personal issues about your marriage are not an area for negotiation—but details about the ceremony and other wedding arrangements certainly could be. Decide to be flexible and accommodating when you can.

Create an Hour of Wedding Silence

During a certain time of your mutual choosing, every day, the two of you should talk about anything: the weather, sports, or politics—anything *except* your wedding. Don't talk about song lists, stay away from discussions about fonts for the invitations, and, for the love of everything good in this world, forget the guest list for a few hours. You can extend this concept a step further and create a weekly date nights—for you two and no one else. Just as you would never bring work from the office on a first date, your weekly date nights should be just as "sacred." The date night is not a time to discuss wedding plans or take cell phone calls from pushy parents.

Secondly, it is essential to take the high road whenever possible. It may be difficult to bite your tongue in response to what you consider rude remarks—and your loved ones can certainly make some comments that hurt your feelings. But realize that most often, that person's intention was not to hurt you; he or she probably just got caught up in the emotions of the moment—something we all do. Try to develop a bad memory, even making the decision to be "hard of hearing," if only for a little while. Recognize that you have the option to take action and prevent grudges from developing or worsening. Isn't it worth it?

Third, remember that no matter what you do, people are responsible for their own actions. There is always a part of us that feels that if we were different in some way, the other person would behave better. That may or may not be true—but you are who you are, and they are who they are. In the end, each individual is only responsible for himself or herself. Remember that if you do have to take a stand, take the high road. There is a big difference between stating your case and standing up for yourself. Try not to react with angry and hurtful words that will, one way or another, come back to haunt you in years to come. It is amazing how one-sided people's memories can be. Years later, they will remember that you reacted with anger, but they will not remember any of their actions that led up to it.

So exactly how do you take the high road but still stand up for yourself? Easy: *state your case—and nothing else.* That means being careful not to bring anything else into the discussion. Talk about you, not your fiancé. Want to bring up her lack of judgment from three years ago? Save it for another time. Want to get in one of your incredibly witty remarks like, "You always have to have your way, right?" Don't. *State your case—and nothing else.* It may sound easy, but it's not. Although it's not easy, it works.

Make an Escape Bag

Sit down together and think of all the things you would like to do for "fun" in an afternoon, a day, or weekend. Write them down on individual cards and label them "hours," "days," or "weekend," depending upon the amount of time that each will take. At least once a week, take a break from wedding planning, and with your eyes closed, choose a card and then do the listed activity. Have fun!

Setting Boundaries

A wedding is a union between two individuals. Yet, the relationship will be healthier if each of you actively maintains the aspects of your personalities that are unique to you. The need to please and accommodate each other that you are feeling now can help identify where boundaries need to be drawn. To do this, you must each look at your own desires, needs, and health first. Then, see where these fit with the needs of each other, as well as those of your family and friends. If there is a big difference between your needs and the needs of others (including your partner's), this may be the sign of a real disconnect or of "unfinished business" from your past that needs to be addressed. For example, your fiancée may not feel it is important for your brother to be a groomsman. However, understanding that you are trying to resolve some childhood issues between you and your brother can be critical in making a wedding decision that will help you become a whole, healed adult.

Boundaries draw a line between who you are and who someone else is. When your identity is yours and no longer relies on rescuing, changing, or controlling another person, you have drawn appropriate boundaries. Communicating your acceptance of each other and asking for each other's acceptance for each of you will help make you feel better about both your plans and decisions together as a couple.

Use Your Brain a Little

The wedding is a good opportunity to test your communication and resolution skills by listening, asking clarifying questions, speaking clearly and non-defensively, and then working toward negotiating a "creative alternative" or compromise solution.

Learn to brainstorm about conflicts and find a solution that works for both of you.

1. Find a problem that needs to be addressed that's not too heavy.
2. Describe the problem.
3. Identify what you are trying to get away from.
4. What would be a perfect way to deal with your problem?
5. Start brainstorming about various solutions. Get outside the box of what you have tended to think about before. (Have fun. Be ridiculous. Can't figure out where to seat everyone?—Maybe you could use a grab bag or let everyone take a number when they get to the reception. Could be interesting!)

Recognizing Stress

Wedding planning can take a toll on your physical, emotional, and relationship well-being. Stress can disrupt a number of your normal response patterns that directly affect the way you think, feel, and react. Keep an eye out for the following behaviors in yourself or your fiancé—they are usually indications that you or the other person are under more stress than you realize:

- **Excessive and compulsive behaviors:** Nail-biting, teeth clenching, overeating, pacing, scratching—or no response at all—to stressful situations.
- **Illogical and incoherent thinking:** Things such as memory loss, the inability to concentrate, repetitive thoughts, nightmares (*your wedding day is here and the caterer, photographer, and florist simultaneously go out of business, etc.*), and the reduced ability to deal with day-to-day problems.
- **Intense and continued negative emotions:** Anger, anxiety, sadness, guilt, or irritability.

Take Time Out From Bad Behavior

Take a look at the things and the times that stress you out the most. You probably think you know what they are; but my guess is that you probably don't know *why* they are turning you into someone even you wouldn't want to marry.

- Log your stressed out behavior by identifying antecedent (i.e., those events that occur right before you freak out). It is probably a good idea to jot these down on paper.
- After a week, look at your list of "antecedents" and see if there are any patterns that you notice. Most likely, you will discover that for many of the events on your list, there is some underlying issue that continually sets off your "freak

outs." For example, you may see that the dry cleaner who ruined your shirt or the car service that was ten minutes late are not the real problems. The real problem may be that you are afraid of being fired; everything and anything that remotely may contribute to you losing your job is the real issue as well as anything that may negatively affect your ability to pay for this wedding freaks you out.

• Address the root cause, *not* the actual event.

Try to Forgive—No One Said You Have to Forget

Although it's often not easy to forgive familial weaknesses and faults, it is worth trying. Everyone heals at a different pace; sooner or later with hope, understanding, and reasonable expectations, relationships will improve. You have a brand new life ahead of you both, and this is a good time to make a new start.

• Look realistically at the challenges you face.
• Let go and give away the need to control everything.
• Share what is going on with each other.
• Focus on what is *truly* important.
• If parents disapprove, remain calm and do not react with anger.
• Talk positively about your soon to be in-laws.
• Keep things in perspective.
• Attempt to remain an adult (no matter what the situation).
• Relax. Have faith that this is good and will work out.

INSIGHTS

PLANNING YOUR WEDDING may not be exactly how you imagined it would be. No one told you that it would be this hard, but also no one ever could describe to you the joy that a good marriage can bring. You may be nervous and afraid and feel that everything you do will in some way affect you later in life (and it will, hopefully all for the best). It is okay to be anxious and to acknowledge that you are. You are allowed to feel any way you want—but try not to behave any way you want (at least, if you want your partner, relatives and friends to show up for the wedding).

This is a perfect time to make a public display of what the two of you see as important in your future roles as husband and wife (and as daughter- and son-in-law, and brother- and sister-in-law). There are so many valuable skills to be learned throughout the process that will benefit you through life; practice them now, and use them forever. This is your day—for you and all of your loved ones to share. Help make the wedding more than a great party or spectacular event; make it a reminder of exactly what "I do" means for each of you.

CONCLUSION

*

OKAY, SO YOU have read the entire book and probably would agree that planning your wedding is definitely not how you imagined it. No one could have prepared you for all the emotional ups and downs, the confusing feelings—never mind the difficult personalities—that you have been dealing with lately. However, I am pretty sure that you are beginning to sense the incredible joy that a good marriage will bring. As a society, as we grow continually more focused on the wedding planning, we tend to also lose sight of the personal meanings and wonderful traditions that signify why people get married in the first place. And I am sure you and your fiancé are recognizing this.

Regardless, if you are reading *Occasional Therapy for the Wedding*, you have at least learned one thing: it is okay to be anxious—and even healthier to acknowledge that you are. You are allowed to feel any way you want (just try not to behave any way you want). Wedding planning is a process of learning and adjusting, just as your marriage—and every stage of your life—will be.

You have no doubt seen what a powerful force the wedding can have, not only for you, but for your entire family (and his). Even though the wedding is all about you (it is, right?), for even the most normal families, the stress that surrounds the wedding may bring out the worse in us: long-standing, delicate relationships get worse; forgotten-about family issues rise anew; trivial details suddenly become urgent; major issues get ignored. Also, our modern society has no doubt thrown some additional challenges at us: with more and more brides and grooms emerging from blended families and stepfamilies, the wedding can present a traditional and communicational challenge as well.

Instead of getting flustered, depressed, or angry, use this time to try to understand yourself, your groom, and your families. Weddings are a time for families to communicate with one another—and should be a time to understand one another's needs, goals, and challenges in life. Events, particularly celebratory ones like a wedding, can offer a time to heal from losses and forgive disappointments.

Always give others the benefit of the doubt; try to take the high road whenever possible and attempt to understand why they see the world the way they do. Consider gender roles and societal expectations and how they play a huge part in how much men and women play in the planning of the wedding. Attempt to understand your parents and how much the "giving away" of the bride to the groom symbolizes their "letting go" of the daughter, and to some extent, their larger familial roles. You are now achieving independence: the wedding marks the beginning of a new nuclear family, and parents' relationships with their children change as a result.

Just as you may be confused, your loved ones (parents, siblings, relatives, even your fiancé) may be experiencing a real sense of loss and separation. However, remember that no matter what you do, people are responsible for their own actions. Try not to react with anger and hurtful words that will, in some way or another, come back to haunt you in the years to come. Keep in mind how one-sided our memories can be. (Years later, others will remember that you reacted with anger, but not their own actions that led up to your outburst.) If you are having problems with his or with her family, remember that acceptance is the key word here. This is the family raised your fiancé, after all, so they must have a lot of good points if you go out of your way to look for them.

By reading *Occasional Therapy for the Wedding* you have a chance to look realistically at the challenges that face everyone involved in the wedding. By recognizing the major causes of your emotions and evaluating your current behavior, you can effectively eliminate irrational beliefs and distorted thinking that leads to unwanted stress. With what you have learned you can try to heal past hurts and experience closeness—in this way, true satisfaction in the new relationship becomes possible. Shifting your perspective can change your expectations of others, which in turn allows a new and different relationship to emerge. Accepting differences in others acknowledges that there may never be agreement on certain subjects and forces concentration on other areas of the relationship.

Always keep in mind that all the frivolous details you have been obsessing over lately are really very superficial appendages to the wedding ritual. Scratch the veneer off the surface, and what you will really discover is that these are just accessories to a larger, public declaration showing which values, traditions, and family members you cherish.

Reading *Occasional Therapy for the Wedding* can help you figure out how to survive the wedding and enjoy it and will provide insights into yourself that will be used to cope with other occasional events (the pregnancy, the in-law holiday visits or the birth of a child). But again, we're getting ahead of ourselves here.

GLOSSARY

Aggression: Hostile behavior intended to cause psychological or physical harm to another individual.

Adjustment: A process of changing behavior in response to the physical, psychological, or social demands of one's self, others, or the environment. An "adjustment period" occurs when an individual is going through a process of change and is searching for some level of balance or acceptance with the environment, others, or himself/herself.

Adjustment disorder: Refers to a psychological disturbance that develops in response to specific sources of stress, such as personal crisis (divorce, death of loved one, recent abuse, recent job changes) or major unexpected negative events (tornado, flood, or fire). Happy major life-cycle events like marriage and pregnancy also can be the cause. When reactions to these events seriously impair social and occupational functioning they are considered a disorder.

Anxiety: Is an unpleasant emotional state that involves a complex combination of emotions that include fear, apprehension, and worry. Emotionally, anxiety causes a sense of dread or panic. These behaviors are frequent and often maladaptive. Anxiety is a common emotion along with fear, anger, sadness, and happiness.

Anxiety disorders: A disorder characterized by excessive, exaggerated anxiety and worry about everyday life events. People with anxiety disorders tend to always expect disaster, and often their worry is unrealistic or out of proportion for the situation.

Behavior modification: The use of learning principles to help people develop more effective and adaptive behaviors, increase the frequency of desired behaviors, or decrease the frequency of problem behaviors.

Catharsis: An emotional release: The process of expressing strongly felt but usually repressed emotions such as anger or aggression—and arriving at "another place" or mental state. ("Venting" anger is an example of cathartic behavior.)

Chronic stress: A continuous state where an individual perceives demands as greater than the inner and outer resources available for dealing with them. Chronic stress is long lasting and can lead to emotional and physical distress.

Cognitive Behavioral Therapy: A psychotherapeutic method used to replace distorted attitudes and problem behavior by modifying everyday thoughts and behaviors. It involves identifying irrational thinking and learning to replace it with more realistic substitute ideas.

Defense mechanisms: A way for the mind to protect individuals from being consciously aware of thoughts or feelings that are too difficult to tolerate; can sometimes trigger a withdrawal response.

Denial: A defense mechanism in which a person unconsciously rejects thoughts, feelings, needs, or external realities that they would not be able to deal with because they are too painful to handle.

Displacement: A defense mechanism whereby a person shifts his impulses from an unacceptable target to a more acceptable or less threatening target. Individuals tend to lash out or display anger at others who are really not the cause of their anger, but with whom they feel emotionally safe.

Empathy: Is an ability to understand and feel what another person is feeling in an emotional sense. Being empathetic helps people to understand another person's situation, perspective, and problems much better.

Empathy is characterized as the ability to "put oneself into another's shoes."

Individuation: Is a process of becoming aware of oneself, of one's makeup, and the way to discover one's true, inner self: defines the struggle to find one's own true personality.

Intellectualization: Is a defense mechanism used to avoid confrontation with an unconscious conflict and its associated emotional stress. *Intellectualizing* is used to avoid uncomfortable emotions by focusing only on facts and logic.

Just-world view: A tendency for people to believe that the world is fair; therefore, people get what they want and deserve what they get.

Panic attacks: Symptoms of anxiety disorders where individuals experience brief episodes of intense sense of extreme fear or psychological distress that prompts severe physical reactions in your body. These attacks generally are not attached to a specific event or object but instead seem to come "from nowhere."

Passive-aggressive: Displaying aggression indirectly, as opposed to directly (hitting, yelling, etc.). There is no direct anger or confrontation involved, but the person expresses aggression indirectly, through stubbornness, procrastination, resentment, intentionally failing to follow through on requested actions, etc.

Projection: A defense mechanism by which people disguise their own threatening impulses by attributing them to others. One ("projects") to others, one's own unacceptable or unwanted thoughts and/or emotions.

Psychotherapy: A treatment of emotional, behavioral, or interpersonal problems through the use of psychological techniques designed to encourage understanding of problems and modify troublesome feelings, behaviors, or relationships. Any of a group of therapies used to treat psychological disorders that focus on changing faulty behaviors, thoughts, perceptions, and emotions that may be associated with specific disorders.

Rationalization: When an individual is unable to deal with the reasons he (or she) behaves in particular ways and protects himself by creating self-justifying explanations for his behaviors. Rationalization is a defense mechanism that offers justifying explanations in place of the real, more threatening, unconscious reasons for one's actions.

Reconstructive memory: Is an active process in which information meant to be remembered, and information from our knowledge and experience of the world are combined. Often what happens is that what we recall is not an accurate reproduction of the original experience.

Regression: A defense mechanism where a person is faced with a situation that is so anxiety provoking that he (or she) cannot deal with it and protects himself by retreating to an earlier stage of development; often carried out at a subconscious level.

Self-actualization: A concept referring to a person's constant striving to reach his talents, capabilities and potential. This is the ultimate psychological need to fulfill one's full potential.

Self-fulfilling prophecy: Is a prediction that one makes about himself that actually causes itself to become true. People may unknowingly react to statements of others, either through fear or logical confusion, and as a result their reactions ultimately fulfill the prophecy of that person.

Stress: A negative emotional state occurring in response to events that are perceived as exceeding more than one can handle; a psychological and physical response of the body occurring whenever a person must adapt to changing conditions.

Stressors: Common psychological stressors evoke distressing emotions, such as hate, anger, sadness, and fear. Physical stressors include everything from lack of sleep to invasive surgery. Stressors can be associated with a positive (a promotion, getting married) or negative event (job loss, divorce).

Social norms: The expectation a group has for its members regarding acceptable and appropriate attitudes and behaviors; rules for the expected behavior in a certain situation.

Type-A behavior pattern: A complex pattern of behaviors and emotions that includes excessive emphasis on competition, aggression, impatience, and hostility.

Type-B behavior pattern: As compared to Type-A behavior pattern, a less competitive, aggressive, or hostile pattern of behavior and emotion.

Unconditional positive regard: Complete, unconditional love and acceptance of an individual by another person, such as a parent has for a child. Also, the sense a person may have that he or she is loved and valued even if he or she does not conform to the standards and expectations of others.

Validation: Is the respect for a communication partner, which involves the acknowledgement that the other person's opinions are legitimate and are valued.

Wellness: Optimal health, incorporating the ability to function fully and actively over the physical, intellectual, emotional, spiritual, social, and environmental domains of health.

RESOURCES

INTERNET

AMERICAN PSYCHIATRIC ASSOCIATION

Healthy Minds. Healthy Lives.

www.healthyminds.org

The American Psychiatric Association provides a resource for mental health information and news through its Web site. The public can access up-to-date information on individual and family mental health needs, resources, and referrals.

ADMINISTRATION FOR CHILDREN AND FAMILIES (ACF)

U.S. Department of Health and Human Services ACF Healthy Marriage Initiative www. acf.dhhs.gov/healthymarriage/index.html

This is the official site of the Administration of Children and Families (ACF) of the U.S. Department of Health and Human Services. It offers pre-marital and marital education resources. Information from the ACF Healthy Marriage Initiative can help couples acquire the skills and knowledge necessary to form and sustain a healthy marriage.

AMERICAN PSYCHOLOGICAL ASSOCIATION (APA)

APA Help Center www.apahelpcenter.org/

The Help Center is a resource for brochures, tips, and articles on the psychological issues that affect physical and emotional well being. Information about referrals to mental health professionals is available.

MAYO CLINIC

www.mayoclinic.com/health/mental-health/MH99999

The Mayo Clinic is the first and largest integrated, not-for-profit group practice in the world. The Web site contains information on mental health and mental illness, specific disorders, and mental health treatments. Strategies to improve individuals' personal mental health are also included.

MENTAL HEALTH AMERICA

www.nmha.org/go/get-info/

Mental Health America (formerly known as the National Mental Health Association) is the country's leading nonprofit dedicated to helping people live mentally healthier lives. Mental Health America's fact sheet "Finding the Right Care" provides detailed information to help patients choose a therapist and enable them to better understand treatment options and the treatment process.

NATIONAL INSTITUTE OF MENTAL HEALTH

U.S. Department of Health and Human Services www.nimh.nih.gov/

The National Institute of Mental Health (NIMH) is a component of the National Institutes of Health (NIH), the federal government's primary research agency; NIH is part of the U.S. Department of Health and Human Services. The "For the Public Section" provides information on symptoms, diagnosis, and treatment of mental disorders, as well as other educational materials.

HOTLINES

The National Suicide Prevention Lifeline's 24-hour toll-free crisis hotline, 1-800-273-TALK (1-800-273-8255) can put you into contact with your local crisis center, which can tell you where to seek immediate help in your area.

OTHER SUGGESTED RESOURCES

- Your local health department's Mental Health Division
- Family physician
- Clergy
- Family social services agencies
- Educational consultants or school counselors
- Marriage and family counselors
- Psychiatric hospitals
- Hotlines, crisis centers, and emergency rooms

DISCLAIMER

While these resources can be helpful, you should discuss specific concerns regarding the diagnosis and treatment of any mental disorders affecting yourself or a family member with your health care provider. The information contained in these Web sites is not intended as, and is not, a substitute for professional medical advice. The author is not responsible for content provided on these Web sites and does not guarantee the accuracy of the information they contain. All decisions about clinical care should be made in consultation with a qualified health care professional.